You Complete Me
AND OTHER MYTHS THAT DESTROY
Happily Ever After

You Complete Me
AND OTHER MYTHS THAT DESTROY
Happily Ever After

VICTORIA FLEMING, PH.D.

NORTH SHORE WELLNESS SERVICES, LTD.
NORTHBROOK, ILLINOIS

Copyright © 2011 by Victoria Fleming

All rights reserved. Published by North Shore Wellness Services, Ltd. No part of this book may be reproduced or transmitted in any form or by any means, electronic or mechanical, including photocopying, recording, or by any information storage and retrieval system, without written permission from the publisher. North Shore Wellness Services, Ltd. • 3000 Dundee Road, Suite 411 • Northbrook, IL 60062

The case studies in this book are fictitious compilations of issues and events commonly encountered in psychotherapy. All names and details have been significantly altered from original source material. Any similarities to any person living or dead is coincidental.

This book is set in 12-point Times New Roman.
Printed in the United States of America
ISBN-13: 978-1-456-31200-8
ISBN-10: 1-456-31200-6

Library of Congress Control Number: 2010918780

www.mythsaboutmarriage.com

An audio recording of this book is available.

To Gary for his unwavering support and encouragement, and to Isabelle and Rosie for helping me keep life in balance.

CONTENTS

Introduction i

Chapter	Myth	Page
1	You Complete Me 1
2	Marriage Will Change Him 15
3	If He Would Be Perfect, I Would Be Happy 29
4	Let's Make a Deal: The Barter Economy Marriage 41
5	We'll Be Happy When We Get There 53
6	Children Will Bring Us Closer Together 67
7	Love Will Keep Us Together 81
8	I Married the Perfect Person 95
9	She Knows Me Better Than I Know Myself 105
10	We Can Go Back To the Way We Were 123
	Index of Key Names and Terms 135
	Index of Case Studies 136

INTRODUCTION

Humans are born more dependent than almost any other member of the animal kingdom. We need to be connected, and our ability to have healthy connections is required for both our individual survival and the perpetuation of our species. You would think something that important would be a bigger part of our formal education. But alas, we get most of our training from our own families, supplemented by what we see on television. No wonder there is so much drama and emotional turmoil everywhere we turn.

When two people willingly stand up in front of friends, families, and coworkers and pronounce before all that *this is it,* each has found in the other a life partner. Whether it is a wedding or commitment ceremony, if it's the first time or the tenth, if they bring the naiveté of youth or the wisdom of age, there is an optimism in that promise. And let's face it, sometimes that optimism is misplaced. After all, it's not uncommon for people to commit to one another in the face of warning signs that all is not well. Still, it's an incredibly courageous step into a shared life, a leap of faith that they will find their own *happily ever after.*

How these people start with such promise and end up so willing to hurt and be hurt by one another is to me tragic, intriguing, and why I wrote this book. And whether the real problems begin before the *I Do's* or well after the honeymoon is over, what each person brings to the relationship, consciously and subconsciously, charts the course of the relationship for better or for worse. Working with couples in their process back to harmony is one of the great joys of my work as a professional counselor. When that process is mired in conflict, hostility, skepticism, and fear, it can be very painful for everyone involved.

Providing help to couples in all stages of the relationship cycle has given me an opportunity to spend a great deal of time thinking about coupling in general, lifelong commitment in particular, and how relationships come to spiral painfully out of control for so many. I am passionate about the work and captivated by the art and science of the human relationship, so I wrote this book and for any number of reasons, you're reading it. Maybe your marriage feels stale, and you're looking for a way to spruce it up, like a *how to* book for the ultimate do-it-yourself home improvement project. Perhaps you are a serial monogamist, tired of going from one failed relationship to the next. Maybe a friend is about to take the leap, and you're looking for a book to serve as a *travel guide* of sorts, like one you would gift to someone about to embark on any big adventure. It could be the marriage of someone you love is in trouble, and you want to better understand what might be going on.

**This book explores the marriage relationship
and the origins of various marital difficulties.**

I believe if more people understood the mechanics of intimacy and discord, they would be more likely to enter marriage with a sober and realistic view about what it can and cannot do, should and should not be, and what is healthy and what is not. The process of entering lifelong commitments is impeded for the huge number of people unwilling to look at themselves and the baggage they carry unnecessarily through life. If left to their own devices, they would live and die with the same blind spots to their ego-, fear-, or shame-driven lives.

When you are married, you bring another human being into all of your *stuff*. You cannot remain oblivious to your blind spots when you have a spouse holding up a mirror. If you're not open to personal growth and change, both yours and your partner's, the outcome of the union will likely be heartache.

If your relationship has gotten stuck or isn't working, perhaps you are in couple's therapy or resisting pressure from your spouse to go. Maybe you harbor secret hope that you'll get what you need here instead. You might, if you are willing to be truly open and honest with yourself about *who you are* as a person and partner. Few people get to that place without help. If you can, kudos. I do invite you to be open to the possibility that what you are about to read may need some interpretation and safe exploration with a professional. Pay attention to material that feels relevant to you, but also take note of what doesn't feel relevant to you. In fact, if anything feels completely outside the realm of human possibility because it is **so** *not like you,* it might be important. In short, if thou dost protest too much, thou might want to take a closer look. We all have blind spots. This book may help you to recognize some of yours.

If you are in the market for this book because of the state of your own relationship, you're likely:

(1) Not happy and seeking help;
(2) Feeling pretty hopeless, but interested in taking one last shot to improve the relationship; or
(3) Coming out of a failed relationship and determined to do it better next time.

This book can benefit you at any of these stages. Moving forward in your journey with a deeper understanding of your *self* will serve you in countless ways, in countless relationships.

For those readers currently in relationships, whether you are happily or unhappily attached, heading to the altar or divorce court, you are likely in one of these groups:

(1) You've been faithful to your partner and never open to the possibility of cheating;
(2) Although technically faithful, you've experienced at least one close call with infidelity, or you've developed important relationships — at work, on line, at the gym — that leave you vulnerable to infidelity;
(3) You've been unfaithful.

And let's just end the suspense right now — internet infidelity *counts.* If you have broken the bond of trust with your mate by going outside the relationship to satisfy your need for intimacy, that's cheating. Don't bother trying to get off on a technicality. This book is about being real, and it starts here.

I won't spend too much time talking about whether or not you've experienced a close call, an opportunity to cheat or develop an inappropriate relationship with someone other than your spouse, because if you're breathing then you have.

"I didn't go looking for this, it just happened."

Those are the words of someone either naive to or in denial about the world in which we live. We have 24-hour access to people, and with the click of a button we can sort through them and almost instantly find those with similar interests or hobbies, who are like-minded politically, socially, or religiously — not to mention our ability to transform ourselves through the keyboard into any avatar we want to be. Thanks to the internet, *everyone* is potentially open for business.

My hope is that this book will inspire you, no matter what group you are in. If it catches you before you've been open to infidelity, you might be awakened and motivated to make the most of your marriage and avoid common pitfalls. If you are in the second group, this book will help you to see the role various relationships play in your life, which would enable you to make conscious choices that bring happiness and peace of mind. If you have already strayed beyond the bounds of fidelity, this book can bring you some understanding as to why and provide a foundation on which you can build a new relationship, either with your current spouse or without, that will be a better match for the *real* you.

Maybe you're reading this book because your spouse is unhappy, and you want to be proactive in addressing the issues. I've worked with men who come in under orders from their wives to get help, sometimes as a couple and sometimes alone. Here's an exchange I had with one such husband who came in alone:

Me: *So what brings you here today?*
Him: *My wife made me come.*
Me: *Oh? So are you here for you or your wife?*
Him: *Well, she sent me with a list of things I need to fix.*

The dreaded Honey-Do P-List: Partnering, parenting, providing, partying, power, and personal hygiene. These are like the lower decks of the Titanic — you can take a hit in one or two, maybe even three, and stay afloat. But if your spouse hits you with four or five categories of complaints, the ship is going to sink. You can try to rearrange the deck chairs, but you're going down. The Honey-Do P-List often provides a cover for the deeper marital issues, which we will address in Chapter 3.

This book explores common myths in relationships. It is written for both men and women. You won't see yourself in every myth, but I am hard-pressed to think of a couple that doesn't live under the assumptions of at least one of them. They aren't all created equal, some are more destructive, and certainly the degree to which they define the relationship can have a major impact on whether or not the couple can live happily with one or several of them.

Ideally, you will find a reading buddy — a trusted confidant — with whom you can explore the myths. This could be your spouse, your therapist, or your best friend, so that you can discuss the myths and how they do and do not manifest in relationships close to you.

A Final Note of Warning: If your relationship is in trouble and only one of you is willing to examine the issues, the relationship is at risk of having asymmetrical growth, and yes, you can keep walking along with the resulting limp, but it may not be comfortable for either of you. Ideally, you will read the book together, work through myths that are present in your relationship, and find your own *happily ever after*.

MYTH 1:
YOU COMPLETE ME

I was in middle school when I first saw a classmate wearing a split heart pendent. I'm sure you've seen one. It's half of a heart and when put next to the other half, the message reads, "True Love," or something equally gushing and, pardon me, *heartfelt*. The subtext of the pendants was pretty clear:

*I am half and my other half is around here somewhere,
not **out there**, hopefully or hypothetically, but actually somewhere
reasonably close by and wearing the other half of my necklace.*

I hadn't thought of those pendants in years, until that scene in *Jerry Maguire* when Tom Cruise dug deep and uttered three words to Renée Zellweger that made hearts swoon: *"You complete me."*

Here's why the notion that *you complete me* sets the stage for failure. *You complete me* trumpets that I am less than whole; I am a mere fraction of whole. Further, *you complete me* announces that I am not whole, but **with you I can be**. Ah, yes, you and I put together will take me from this fraction state to *being* whole. Like the two halves of the pendant, you and I are a perfect fit of two halves.

$$\frac{1}{2} + \frac{1}{2} = 1$$

If we only needed to end up with one person, then this metaphor would be fine. But *you complete me* only works if one partner is willing to surrender their half entirely, and humans don't work that way.

Each person needs to be complete and strives to be whole. It's dynamic. Simply put, if we're going to equate relationships to mathematics, we have to use multiplication. If I need your half and you need mine, we are each trying to take from the other, and we both end up with less than when we started.

½ x ½ = ¼

Notice, too, that even if we start with one healthy, whole person, when paired with someone less than whole, the result is less than one.

1 x ½ = ½

This equation doesn't exist in the real world, because a genuinely whole person wouldn't choose a life mate who isn't whole. Many people *think* they are whole, but their truth is revealed by their choices. A person chooses a partner who "needs fixing" because they derive self-worth through helping others, or they choose a controlling person because they want to avoid taking personal responsibility for themselves or their actions. The bottom line is:

***If I am looking for the rest of me within someone else,
I am setting myself and my relationship up for failure.***

How do we get to this fraction state, and how does it relate to my choice of partners? Let's start with a basic personality psychology that asserts people are born whole, with the full range of their personality potential lying in wait for the developmental process to unfold.

PERSONALITY BASICS

Think about your best friend and describe his or her personality using three adjectives. Is she kind? Stubborn? Trustworthy? Now do the same exercise for a coworker you don't particularly care for. Same list of attributes or different? Think about what you are really describing: *personality.* You are summarizing what you think of a person based on behaviors you've witnessed or heard about through the grapevine. We tend to think of *personality* as a fairly enduring collection of characteristics that includes **traits,** which are pretty stable over time and from one situation to the next, and **states,** which are temporary and dependant on circumstance.

> *"Katie's normally very sensible* (trait) *but seeing that mouse made her hysterical* (state).*"*

When we think of someone's personality, we quickly combine all we know about her and generate shortcuts, *labels,* which help us convey our understanding. We think of Katie first and then we assert that Katie is *sensible.* It also works the other way. Let's say you heard a teaser on the news that a well-known celebrity punched out a reporter. Would you guess it was Tom Hanks? Probably not, because that behavior doesn't fit your impression of his personality. Are people more than this collection of attributes? Of course! When we talk about *personality,* we are really talking about a narrow range of the person's behavior that comes out at certain times under certain circumstances. Keep that in mind as I invite you to look more closely at your own *personality.*

THE ORIGINS OF *PERSONALITY*

There is research and debate in the scientific community as to how *personalities* come to be. Here is a pretty well accepted explanation:

> *Personality, the totality of a person's qualities and traits, is rooted in a genetic predisposition, which is then influenced by environmental variables during the lifespan.*

Personality traits (e.g., kindness, stubbornness, extraversion, passivity), are somewhat hard wired at birth. In other words, we are born with tendencies towards certain characteristics. However, that genetic predisposition only establishes a range of what is possible. A number of factors, such as how we are raised and our cultural mores and norms, influence how traits actually develop. We shouldn't overlook the influence of maturation. Our behavior changes as we grow up, because we develop self-awareness and regulation skills, and we learn what is acceptable in given settings. In fact, the *setting* is often an underappreciated determinant of behavior. For example, people at church tend to behave very predictably, as do people at school, the movies, or work. Different aspects of your *self* show up depending on your stage in life, where you are, and what you're doing. Coworkers might think you are very serious and responsible, while college buddies have a very different impression of you. Think of a typical wedding, when the betrothed gathers into one place different people who mesh with their different *selves* from these different stages. Friends from childhood, professional colleagues, relatives, and college roommates all gathered in the same place at the same time. Watching these groups collide can be more entertaining than the band.

A WORD OF CAUTION

It is easy to misjudge how well we know others. After all, we only see people for a small bit of time out of the day or week, and usually in a specific setting. You may think you know a coworker, a nice guy, pretty laid back at meetings, only to find out he's been arrested for domestic abuse. You did not know him as well as you thought you did because you were only exposed to a specific part of him — his *work self*. On the flip side, you may remember your sibling as a liar who would say anything to avoid getting in trouble, but growing up may have changed those qualities. Your brothers and sisters may be very different now. Getting reacquainted with adult siblings can be very surprising.

Among some of the truths about *personality* you will find:

- Personalities are always more complicated than they first appear.
- There is a mismatch between how we describe someone and how he describes himself, because he has blind spots to aspects of himself and because we do not really know him as well as we think we do.
- The reverse is also true: It might surprise you to learn how the people in your life describe you.
- It is natural to have different aspects of personality come out in different settings. You act very differently in a movie theater than you do in a football stadium.

DESCRIBING YOUR *SELF*

Although different settings and different stages in your life will encourage or discourage various personality characteristics, there is a common thread that links them all together, and that is the **whole** you. Your *sense of self* has continuity to it, and so **you** are in the best position to describe who you are in relation to who you've been in the past and why you currently behave as you do. That doesn't mean you always take full advantage of this unique position. On the contrary, we all have blind spots to our *selves,* and the challenge is to work through our defenses to get to a deeper level of self-awareness. People don't usually spend too much time thinking about their personalities, let alone the *origins* of their personalities, other than to say, *"I get that from my dad,"* or *"I'm just like my mom that way."*

Let's take the example of *assertiveness*, which we can put on a continuum from very little (passive) to a lot (aggressive). We each have the potential to be passive and aggressive. We carry both states within our *selves,* and each is available for use as situations demand. Together, the halves represent the "whole" trait. In short, we can express either state (passive or aggressive), depending on the situation. We can be passive when soothing a tired baby and aggressive when hailing a cab. There's no conflict here. Each state is available for use when the situation calls for it.

Likewise, we can be generous and stingy; happy and sad; extraverted and introverted. There are almost countless personality traits we can divide in this way, and we can demonstrate a wide variety of behaviors depending on many variables, including situation, timing, and mood.

Take a moment to identify three of your more stable personality characteristics.

1._____ 2._____ 3._____

If you had trouble doing this, you are not alone. I am always surprised by how many people have difficulty with this simple exercise. You might worry that a label will limit how the world sees you or how you see yourself. *I don't know. I can be passive sometimes and aggressive at others.* How are you on decisiveness? Maybe you feel that's being tested here. Fear not! Everyone has many aspects to their personalities, and most reassuringly, our personality only identifies our *tendencies* for behavior. We still have *free will* that allows us to be who we want to be in any given situation. So, although I may have some personality characteristics I wish I did not have, those traits don't necessarily impair me.

For example, maybe "quick tempered" is on your list, but you have learned to relax under stress and you don't often indulge your temper. I encourage you to open up to what characteristics most *accurately* describe you, whether you like them or not. If it helps, start by writing down words you think would generate consensus from the people who you know and love you best. Then decide which words you will keep and which you will swap out for words that better describe the *real* you.

How Others See Me	How I See Myself
_____	_____
_____	_____
_____	_____

The extent to which your lists are similar reveals how *real* you are with other people. If your lists are wildly different, stop to think about why. Do you feel you need to behave a certain way with certain people to gain their acceptance? This could be important.

BEING HONEST ABOUT YOUR PERSONALITY

Some people are very self-critical and only identify their worst attributes, which might indicate modesty or low self-esteem. On the other hand, it is natural to be biased in your favor, and recall examples that support only your best self-image. I remember a client whose wife accused him of being tight with money. He defended himself.

> *"I am generous. I gave some change to a guy getting on the bus in front of me just yesterday. He was short, and I had enough. It was the least I could do."*

What's good for therapeutic process may bruise the ego. In our session, his wife offered this rebuttal:

> *"Yes, but you're usually stingy! Last week at the mall we had to drive around to an entrance that didn't have a bell ringing Santa! You only gave that guy your change because he was holding up the line and you didn't want to be late for your meeting!"*

It is natural to get a little cranky when someone holds up a mirror like this. We have a certain image of our selves, and we don't like that image to be contradicted. Have a little huff, take a deep breath, and then get down to the business of exploring this aspect of your personality. See it as an opportunity for growth rather than a threat.

Let's get back to our example of *passive* and *aggressive*. If it is hard for you to hail a cab and easy for you to sooth that baby, would it bother you to be called *passive*? If so, why? Maybe you were truly hardwired to be more passive. Still, you were born capable of expressing passivity *and* aggression, with the potential to behave appropriately in both situations. Maybe that explains our natural aversion to being pigeonholed with labels. They imply limitations that are not necessarily true. Plus, we just don't like people telling us who we are.

THE SHAPING OF YOUR *SELF*

In order to proclaim *"You Complete Me,"* you have to have some sense of who you are and what you're missing. We have already mentioned a number of factors that influence *personality* in general, but how do we end up with *missing parts?* For that, we turn our attention to the early childhood environment. To put it simply,

How I was born + How I was treated = How I approach the world

Admittedly, this is incredibly over-simplified. *How I approach the world* is influenced by hundreds, if not thousands, of variables that include everything from the weather to what I ate for dinner last night. In this context, it is really capturing my personality's "default setting" — am I generally optimistic? Humorous? Shy?

Additionally, understanding the shaping of *self* gets very messy when you consider that people and their environments are "mutually influential," meaning that each influences the other, even in infancy. For example, colicky babies create additional stress in their homes, which in turn influences how adults interact with them. Anxious, first-time parents tend to provide a more stressful environment for babies than seasoned parents. Siblings influence the availability of parents to newborns. Maybe babies cannot grasp the complexities of human relationships, but they smile more at adults who smile back, and they offer "sympathy cries" when they hear other babies crying. Infants clearly connect to their world, and within the first year, they even have a pretty good sense of cause and effect. Dropping something on the floor and watching mom pick it up and return it to the highchair tray is a great game. *I do this and she does that ... again, and again, and again!* It's a game, but if the parent doesn't understand that — if she believes the baby is being annoying on purpose and scolds the baby or isolates her in a time out — the baby has *learned* that playing will be punished.

As time goes on, babies become toddlers who have begun to *adapt* to the demands of their environment. This *adaptation,* which continues throughout childhood, is what leads to the development of certain aspects of our *selves.* If one way of responding — one state — helped you cope with your environment growing up, then it would have flourished while its opposite failed to thrive. In short, personality traits (and the behaviors that represent them) develop in response to your experience in your family of origin, by your primary caregivers, during your formative years. *If I* learn *that behavior I think is playful gets me punished, I'll adapt to that punishment by squelching my playfulness.*

If the environment is sufficiently harsh — judgmental, critical, unloving, or conditional in extending love — you may actually *banish* parts of your *self* that cause problems for you and *embrace* parts that are rewarded with love and acceptance, or at least attention — and at the *very* least, get your basic needs met. Think of "punished" in pure *psychologese* — *anything that decreases behavior is punishing.* It can involve the presentation of something you don't like (e.g., yelling or spanking) or the removal of something you do like (e.g., TV, love, or attention). So, if your aggressive behavior was unacceptable in your family and you were punished for it, you learned to get your needs met in other (more passive and perhaps manipulative) ways. Likewise, if you're from a family in which you had to yell and scream to be heard, you suppressed (punished) the "bad" part of you (the quiet/calm) that didn't get you anywhere, and developed the more aggressive parts of you that were rewarded with getting your needs met.

In some ways, you're off the hook for whatever parts of your personality create challenges for you interpersonally. *Hey, you were just trying to get your basic needs met, after all.* Well, it's not quite that simple. Now that you are an adult, it's time to take responsibility for your *self* and the dominant aspects of your personality.

There are countless personality traits we can split, but here are a few that often manifest in marital difficulties:

> Logical -------------------------- Emotional
> Frugal ---------------------------- Frivolous
> Calm -------------------------------- Anxious
> Introverted --------------------Extraverted

Let's look at Evan and Marguerite, as an example of the *"You Complete Me"* myth in marriage.

Marguerite and Evan: ½ x ½ = ¼

Marguerite came in for counseling with her husband Evan because she was tired of doing all of the emotional heavy lifting in the relationship. She just couldn't get a reaction out of him. Their dance[1] had become clear: He was emotionally very controlling and distancing, while she acted out in an effort to get him to engage. Evan was by all accounts a nice man and a good provider, and he was baffled by Marguerite's hysteria over this issue. From his perspective, there was just no need to get so emotional. He couldn't take her screaming fits anymore, but when he tried to disengage from a fight, she just got nastier, calling him names, swearing, and turning it into a personal attack. They were both miserable.

In Evan's home growing up, he was never overtly punished for being emotional. Punishment would have required some emotional get-up-and-go from his very docile parents. Instead, they ignored emotionality and praised control and intellectualization. Evan's parents engaged with him and responded positively to logic and reason-

---

[1] Harriet Lerner, Ph.D., offers a series of books on interpersonal relationships. *Dance of Anger* is a book I recommend to many couples. *Dance of Fear, Dance of Deception,* and *Dance of Intimacy* are also good picks you can find at most bookstores.

ing. He learned very quickly how to behave to get his parents' acceptance, and he banished the emotional parts of himself that didn't.

In Marguerite's home, the opposite was true. It was easy to get lost in her loud, Greek family. If you didn't shout, you weren't heard, and if you weren't heard, you didn't get any attention at all. Marguerite learned very young that loud is "good" and quiet is "bad."

When Marguerite met Evan, he was just what she needed in her life. She had always been very emotional and impulsive, and a bit of a drifter when it came to jobs and money. She had continued to live a college lifestyle, renting an apartment and temping for a local agency, until she met Evan on her 30th birthday. She thought it was a sign. He really had his act together — job, home, savings. Evan had everything she found unattainable in her own life. As for Evan, Marguerite was like a breath of fresh air. He loved her free-spirited nature, and he couldn't believe she was attracted to him.

Notice how parents rewarded and punished Marguerite and Evan's emotions during their formative years. For Evan, emotionality was simply ignored while the logical-reasoning part of him was rewarded, and the net effect was the same — the expression of the characteristic that was rewarded with attention or love and the banishment of its opposite. Marguerite's family ignored her when she was unemotional, so she banished that and developed a tendency to be emotional. Take a moment to think about this idea. We are born whole and capable of expressing the full range of any given trait. When we are inclined to express a trait, but find that by doing so we experience punishment *(i.e., an aversive consequence)* from the people who feed and love us, we banish that part of our *selves*. **Banishment.** We send it away, into the deep recesses of the mind. Gone. Rejected. Not welcome. And we're *little* when we do this. Think of a young child so afraid of losing the affection of his parents that he learns to hate an aspect of his personality. This is huge. If you're a fast reader, slow down, take a breath, and really consider the following. No matter how certain the punishment or rejection by the parents, the truth is

No one can banish or exile your parts except you!

You may resist this notion for very rational reasons. After all, if parents are in effect punishing certain aspects of you, certainly they are to blame. And indeed, parents hold significant *influence* over which parts we banish. Still, we are the only ones who banish, therefore,

We are the ONLY ones who can restore our banished parts.

This is an important concept to believe in order to open yourself up to your personal responsibility to restore yourself to whole and to accept the power you possess to do so. *You made the shift to exclude that part of you, and only you can shift back!*

In short, Evan had banished the part of him that didn't get him the love he needed from his parents. Hated it. Rejected it. But ultimately, that banished part was a part of him. In fact, it was a part of him he was originally inclined to express. He only banished it to secure his good standing with his parents. It's *still* a part of him, and a part that he subconsciously misses. Let's fast forward to adulthood, when he met a woman who exuded this missing emotional part of himself. He entered the relationship feeling Marguerite completed him, and, in a deep psychological sense, he was right. The part that he disallowed to exist in himself he found in her. *It was the very recognition of the missing part that drew him to her in the first place!* This same process was at work for Marguerite. She had banished her grounded and quiet parts, which she found in Evan.

ature *You Complete Me* is really the restoration of a missing part of my banished self.

The problems emerge because we banish parts for a reason. In the mind of the developing child, the part was *bad*. It threatened the child's good standing with the parent so he learned to hate it. He banished it in order to protect that relationship. As an adult, the deeply held subconscious belief that the part is *bad* is eventually what causes the marriage issues. Evan, like we all would, came to hate those *bad* qualities in Marguerite the same way he hated them in himself. And it gets worse. Not only is he living with a life-size manifestation of his banished self, but **he has become the oppressive parent,** trying to punish and control the very qualities that drew him into the relationship. *Just as he had those qualities squashed by his parents, he is now trying to squash those qualities in his partner.*

THE ROAD BACK TO WHOLE

The goal is for each person to find their own whole self, so that neither one is trying to extract any missing parts from the other. This is certainly easier said than done. Nevertheless, when they are both whole, then they can look at each other and determine if the relationship is a good fit. Notice, too, that even our mathematical equation works if each person enters the relationship in a state of being whole:

$1 \times 1 = 1$

Two healthy and whole people *can* make one healthy and whole relationship. Evan and Marguerite each needed to acknowledge their banished parts. For Marguerite, whose background included emotionality and chaos, she needed to find her own peaceful center, and she needed to learn that she *could* get her needs met without yelling. She worked hard to develop emotional regulation tools and take responsibility for her behavior. Evan needed to develop self-confidence and strengthen his belief that he could be emotional without driving people away. They entered therapy as two halves of the whole emotional picture. What worked as a romantic notion in the early part of the relationship *(You complete me, you are my missing part)*, had turned into the primary issue *(Now I remember why I ditched that part of me to begin with!)*. They started to work on their individual issues, welcoming back their banished parts. In essence, they each worked toward being complete.

Evan began taking a more proactive approach around the house and with the children. Once he began to see that Marguerite's emotions were coming from her fears, he actually had a lot of compassion for her. He no longer personalized her tantrums, and so he could stay on task without indulging her emotional chaos. Whenever she did yell at him or call him names, rather than a hasty and silent retreat, he used his words, owned his feelings, and left the room. They worked hard to create and maintain healthy boundaries with each other. He wouldn't leave the room as long as her fit was directed at the issue and not targeted towards him. She would leave him alone when he left the room with the understanding that he would come back when she was under control.

Over time, his acceptance of her emotional states increased, but her need to be so emotional decreased. They found a balance that worked for them.

Towards the end of our work together, she happily conveyed a story to me about how he had handled a recent crisis with one of their children. He expressed how pleased he was with her, because she let him handle it without jumping in and taking over. Each had developed a trust of and appreciation for the other, while feeling the benefits of welcoming back their own banished parts. When they were each whole, they had a new marriage that satisfied them both.

CONCLUSION

We have addressed the origins of personality, paying particular attention to how various aspects of our character were encouraged or discouraged by our families of origin. Owning all of your parts, welcoming them back into your behavioral repertoire, is an important step towards being whole.

You Complete Me is a lovely, romantic, and ultimately destructive notion. Finding a partner you feel *completes you* offers an opportunity for personal growth that can actually strengthen a relationship, but it must first start with a deep and personal exploration about what is missing in you.

MYTH 2:
MARRIAGE WILL CHANGE HIM

The human brain is a fascinating organ. Because we are bombarded by much more stimuli in our environment[2] than we could possibly deal with consciously, the brain creates shortcuts and allows us to ignore whatever it deems to be unimportant at the moment. Pause for a few seconds right now and become aware of noises around you. Can you hear the tick of a clock? The whir of a fan? The slosh of a washing machine? The brain takes it all in, but we *adapt* to extraneous sounds so we can channel our conscious attention to whatever is more important, like reading this book. Our brains are also very good at constructing wholes from parts on our behalf. When we look at a table, we don't see lines, angles, and surfaces as separate entities; we perceive a single table, and we have a pretty good idea about what it can do. It will support my coffee cup and the weight of my elbows as I lean over and read the paper. Our brains also offer shortcuts in the form of *scripts* about how relationships work.

---

[2] The environment includes the *external* environment, the physical world in which we live, and the *internal* environment of the human body. Our brains allow our adaptation to stimuli coming from both. For example, wiggle your toes right now. Drawing attention to your foot brings you from an adapted state to a state of awareness. *"Hey, I have a foot and I can feel it in my shoe!"* Our internal stimuli alone would provide a debilitating amount of stimuli were it not for our brain's amazing ability to adapt.

ALL ABOUT SCRIPTS

We have scripts about how mothers and daughters are supposed to interact, how doctors and patients should relate to one another, and how love and marriage is supposed to play out. Our scripts can be so strong, they actually block us from seeing what's real.

Rebecca and Jesse: The Power of the Script
Rebecca was a senior in high school when a popular athlete took an interest in her. At eighteen, Jesse had it all: a part-time job that paid well, a cool car, and good hair. She was over the moon. The two continued to date while Rebecca was away at college. During that time, Jesse's part-time job turned into full-time employment. In his spare time, he liked to work on cars and hang out with friends. He started a weekly card game with some high school buddies and regularly stopped at a local bar on his way home from work. Rebecca visited from college as often as she could. She thought Jesse was a real diamond in the rough. With a little polishing, he would be perfect. There was tension around the amount of time he spent with friends and how he spent his money, but on balance, the thrill outweighed the doubts. She graduated from college, moved back to town, and they dated for two more years. They got married because, as she put it, "We had invested nearly seven years together. It was time to either break up or get married."
By the time they came in for counseling, they had been married ten years and had three children, ages eight, six, and three. Rebecca was a full-time account manager by day and a full-time homemaker whenever she wasn't at work. Between the house and the children, there was always work to be done. Rebecca could have been more forgiving of how little Jesse did around the house were he more successful at work. In fact, she'd grown increasingly frustrated by Jesse's lack of career ambition. He passed up several opportunities to advance to management in the company he'd been with for fifteen years. He coached his son's little league team, but didn't have much to do with either of his daughters. He still played in a weekly card game and stopped for drinks after work, but what put Rebecca over the top was her discovery of inappropriate text messages on Jesse's cell phone from a new receptionist at his company. Although flirta-

tious in nature and inappropriate, they did not evidence infidelity. Still, Rebecca had reached the end of her rope.

Jesse was also fed up with their relationship. He complained Rebecca never had time for him. He didn't mind her having a career, he enjoyed the extra money, but Rebecca hardly ever cooked, she neglected the laundry, and she never seemed interested in being alone with him. Any spare time she had, she spent with the kids. He was tired of being last on the list. "Even the dog outranks me," he lamented.

Rebecca and Jesse, as we all do, entered adulthood with *scripts,* preconceived notions, about marriage. Although Rebecca and Jesse were not particularly mindful of these scripts, their brains filtered information to suit subconscious expectations written in them. They paid attention to things that fit their scripts and ignored things that didn't. For example, Rebecca's script for HUSBAND AND FATHER was a gainfully employed man who climbs the corporate ladder towards comfortable retirement. Although gainfully employed, Jesse lacked career ambition, but because in her script, *"husbands have career ambition,"* she ignored this fact about Jesse early on. Jesse's script for WIFE AND MOTHER was very clear. It was her job to attend to the house and children. Whatever else she wanted to do was sort of beyond the point. The fact that, *"Rebecca had career ambitions,"* which would prevent her from fulfilling his subconscious script, wasn't really on his radar until the pain of the inconsistency could no longer be ignored.

We write our marriage scripts during our formative years, based on a variety of relationship models we see in our family, community, and in the media. Some parts of the scripts are conscious and others are subconscious. When asked about what she expected from marriage, Rebecca spoke from her conscious script. Marriage involved certain roles and expectations about what was to be: A tic-wearing husband who conquers the corporate world by day and dutifully makes it home for dinner each evening; happy, healthy, able-bodied children; a pleasing house with a nice yard; a well-groomed and well-trained pet, carpools, family dinners, the evening news. It was clear Jesse didn't slot into this scene, and frankly, her own ambitions weren't part of it, either. Yet, she took the script for granted. It was more powerful than life, because in reality, she was dating a good guy with a sense of humor who was neither ambitious nor particularly devoted to her. Yet, when she pictured the kind of *husband* he would be, her script shaped her belief that he would emerge from the honeymoon as a go-getter and devotional, in short, one who fit her image, a combination of her own father and Mike Brady. I refer to this as the *Johnny Bravo*[3] approach to spouse selection. *The time is right and you find a guy who fits the suit.*

EDITING THE SCRIPT

Jesse and Rebecca had a seven-year courtship to figure out their scripts didn't match reality, and it still wasn't enough time. They continued to see what they wanted to see in each other. This is called *projection,* and we all tend to do it. The catch is *finding out* that's what we're doing. The brain is taking shortcuts and filtering information. *That's what brains do!* It takes a special metacognition — thinking about our own thinking — to thwart the brain's natural inclination to see what it wants to see. Especially if you still want the fairytale, when you find someone *good on paper* — handsome, wants children, nice income and all that comes with that (home, yard, vacations) — you are motivated to ignore unpleasant *truths.* He drinks, gambles, flirts, cheats on his taxes or on you. Let the mind games begin! You are likely to contort your thinking with a myriad of mental gymnastics in order to avoid reality and take what you believe to be your best shot at *happily ever after.*

People living under the spell of this myth may not realize it until after they have made a commitment and children are involved. Still, when this myth is in play, there are usually signs before the wedding. Excuses a person makes about his or her partner's behavior might resemble one of the following sentences:

---

[3]Johnny Bravo refers to an episode of the Brady Bunch in which Greg Brady was offered a record contract as a solo artist named "Johnny Bravo" (much to the dismay of the whole family and Marcia in particular). They all believed he had been selected because he was so talented and special, but it turned out the record company had already purchased a costume for "Johnny Bravo," and Greg happened to fit the suit. His selection had nothing to do with the attributes that really mattered!

"He does that now because he's single. Once we are married he'll be different."
"She lies at work because she can get away with it. She would never lie to me!"
"He would never treat me the way he treats his (mom, ex, secretary)."

    Maybe you can recall making such excuses for your partner, and in hindsight, you wonder why you did. Maybe you continue to make these excuses in your current relationship. It's important to see past your scripts and embrace the reality of the situation, whatever that may be. Only then will you be positioned to make good, conscious choices for yourself. I recall one client who experienced a real awakening to her script, and she wondered why it took her so long to see the obvious disconnects between reality and what she thought was real. Bewildered, she asked, *"Why in the world has no one pointed this out to me before?"* Chances are no one was willing to raise the tough questions with her. Coworkers and friends likely didn't feel it was their place to do so and offered no more than the mildest raised eyebrow, certainly not enough to shake her out of blissful denial. Family members, especially parents and siblings, who might have been more inclined to ask pointed questions, she dismissed because of their history of criticism. *"I do remember my sister wondering about him,"* she later admitted. *"I thought she was just jealous."*

    On the other hand, maybe you find that your partner makes excuses for your behavior. Do you feel any pressure to change, to conform to a standard he has set for you? This can also lead to a painful realization that perhaps the two of you are not a good match for each other, which is why we tend to ignore or reject such messages. It's an interesting contradiction: *Marriage will fix his problems, but he'd better not think* I'm *going to change!*

    Of course, in reality there are dozens of factors that could potentially interfere with the script. You might fall in love with a member of the same sex, learn you cannot have children, discover you cannot afford a house with a yard, have a pet allergy. There are countless reasons this marital script isn't going to play out as written. Fortunately, you can edit your script, as Abby learns in our next case.

Abby Edits the Script

Abby came from a strong and stable family in which roles were very clear. "Women married young and men provided." She was offered a university scholarship for track and field, which her family supported. Her excitement to go away to college overshadowed her scripted plan to stay home and marry her boyfriend. When undergraduate success earned her a scholarship to a doctoral program, her family was less enthusiastic because they didn't understand why she needed more school. The long-distance relationship with her boyfriend ended as she moved further away from home.

As her twenties came to a close, she was finishing her post-doc and engaged to a fellow graduate student. The two were in the job market for university positions, and one opened up for her first. According to her subconscious script, she was supposed to be at the tail end of having babies by now. Launching a full-time career and marrying a house-husband was straying a bit far off script. Still, she was in love, and she had worked hard for this career opportunity. During her first year on the job, she developed some OCD[4] symptoms. Consciously, she had no idea why she was so anxious, and she attributed it to stress. Five years later, she continued to provide her young family with the primary income and benefits, while her husband worked part-time at a local research lab, scheduling his time around the needs of their young twins.

By the time they came in for therapy, Abby's OCD symptoms had gotten worse. She was critical of her husband and sarcastic about him "wearing the dress in the family." Her logical brain understood that she was an active participant in setting their course, and yet, the subconscious pull to follow the script of a "normal" marriage created this internal conflict, cognitive dissonance, that had a severe impact on her. This subconscious wound festered into bigger and bigger issues until the marriage was really in trouble, each person feeling frustrated and bewildered about what went wrong.

---

[4]OCD stands for Obsessive Compulsive Disorder, a condition marked by extreme anxiety that manifests as persistent and intrusive worrying. To alleviate the anxiety, the person engages in repetitive thoughts or behaviors, such as repeating words, counting, checking locks, washing hands, flipping switches, etc.

Abby's subconscious script sabotaged a perfectly workable arrangement. Through the course of marital work supplemented by intense individual therapy, Abby came to accept that her anxiety was a function of her subconscious expectations, rooted in her past. She brought her script to light and began the process of rewriting. Eventually, she was able to gently but firmly confront the judgmental parts of herself and embrace the life she and her husband had co-created. She became fascinated by her own inconsistencies of feeling. For example, one day she returned home after a really positive and productive work day, very fulfilled by her professional accomplishments. She found a hot meal and happy children waiting for her, thanks to her husband. Before she could enjoy it, a very critical voice in her head questioned *what kind of "real man" plays house-mommy all day long*. This was not coming from her current self, as she was consciously grateful for his flexible schedule and strong parenting skills. As we had practiced in the office, she closed her eyes, took a deep breath, and asked:

*"How old might I be when I **first** feel like there's anything wrong with this picture?"*

This question prompts the body and mind to regress to an earlier experience, and for Abby, she instantly recalled a scene from her childhood. She was eight or nine at the time, sitting around the kitchen table during a big family gathering. Her dad and uncles were laughing and joking, making fun of men who can't keep their women in line. She remembered laughing along with them, wanting to be accepted by them. This insight allowed her to distinguish ***her*** feelings from the feelings of these relatives, and she could make a conscious choice to affirm herself and let go of the maladaptive messages from them, which she had been carrying all this time.

AVOIDING THE SCRIPT-DRIVEN PIT FALLS

Human development involves growth and change and continues through the lifespan, and so yes, technically the person you marry today will be different in the future, as will you be. But, if you aspire to be the primary influence that shapes your partner's development; if you believe — consciously or subconsciously — that you are somehow in control of this process, that you can *control* their developmental course or outcome, then you're setting yourself up for heartbreak and frustration. The power struggle is inevitable. Recall in our first case how Rebecca wanted Jesse to be more successful professionally. In their marriage, she *encouraged* him by urging him to attend training courses, buying him suits and ties on his birthdays, and working "career plans" into many conversations. She did all of this believing she could steer him in that direction. Jesse had no intention of doing more than the bare minimum at work, and he perceived her "encouragement" as nagging.

Your script can also be destructive if it predicts a natural decline in your marriage. For example, many people believe that marriage will naturally get old and stale over time. If this is part of your script and you allow this "truth" to go unchecked, it will become a self-fulfilling prophecy. It doesn't have to. Contrary to what many believe, marriage does not necessarily grow stale. You *can* rewrite your script as you go. Many couples enjoy continued renewal of energy and zest for each other, welcoming each life stage as an opportunity for new experiences and interpersonal growth. Single becomes married. Person becomes parent. Parent becomes grandparent. Life's transitions provide plenty of opportunity to explore new aspects of *self*. Take advantage of every one of them.

Finally, if your script says it's okay to sit around with friends complaining about your marriage, stop and think about how destructive that is. Consider making some serious revisions to your script and with your friends. Several years ago, I attended an inspiring presentation by Les Brown, and I recall his very pointed message about friends. To paraphrase, he said:

If you are the smartest or most successful one in your group, you need to get a different group!

It was funny to hear put so bluntly, but his point is right on. You should surround yourself with people who inspire you to be your best self, with people who *raise the bar* a little. If you hang with people who sit around complaining about marriage, those negative messages will bring you down. Find friends with good marriages. Seek out role model relationships that will inspire you to make the most of your own. Don't settle for company that supports the *"old ball-n-chain"* mentality. Demand more from your friends and better messages for yourself!

DEVELOPING YOUR SCRIPT FOR THERAPY

Let's say reading this chapter has inspired you to rewrite your scripts because, ultimately, you love your spouse and you want to continue doing so. You need some help, but perhaps you hesitate to give counseling a shot because, having never given it much thought, you don't have a script for it. Maybe your "therapy" script is based on what you've seen on television, and you expect it will go like this:

Doctor: *Hello, I am Doctor Soandso. Tell me what is troubling you today.*
Patient: *Well, it all began when I was a teenager . . .*

The patient continues to tell her story while the doctor listens, nods, and eventually offers the single insight that will change her perspective and her life.

It just doesn't happen this way in real life. For those readers new to counseling, I am going to describe what you can expect as you get started. Keep in mind, the process can vary widely depending on the circumstances, but what follows is pretty typical if you seek help from a private practitioner.

Finding a Therapist
It used to be that someone in need of help would ask a trusted confidant or their doctor for a personal referral. Not anymore. People tend to find therapists through their insurance companies or web search engines. Many therapists have web pages that contain much of the basic information you need at this point. If you search for "Counseling in (name your city)," a list of practitioners will appear. Click onto their web pages and you will often find their office hours, fees, insurance they accept, and their areas of specialization. You can usu-

ally eliminate many simply by viewing this information from the comfort of your own home.

Setting up the appointment
Once you have narrowed your list to a few possible therapists, take time to call them, and talk with them briefly on the phone. Not sure what to say? Keep it simple:

"I am looking for a therapist and I came across your name. I am calling to find out if we might be able to work together."

As the 5 to 10 minute conversation unfolds, be aware of how comfortable you feel with their phone mannerisms. If you are comfortable, then you can determine if you and the therapist are available to meet at a mutually agreeable time. Have your exit strategy planned to get off the telephone, so you don't feel pressured to make an appointment if you're not ready.

"Thank you for your time. I am calling a few therapists today, and I will get back to you if I want to set up an appointment."

After you have spoken briefly to several therapists, pick the one you think was the best fit for you, and call to schedule your first appointment, the *intake*.

When setting up the initial session, a therapist should not ask you to commit to more than one visit.

The Intake Session
The ultimate goal of the *intake* session is to find out if the two of you are a good match for the work. The agenda is very packed, as you must address matters of confidentiality, safety, payment, schedule, and therapeutic goals. Most importantly, you both have to determine if you will be able to form what's called a *therapeutic alliance,* which can be summarized in these two questions:

> Practitioner: *"Can I help this person?"*
> Client: *"Can I trust this person?"*

By the end of the intake appointment, each should have a pretty clear answer, and if either answer is "no," you should not schedule a second appointment. Tune into your feelings during the session. *Do I feel comfortable in this place? Do I feel comfortable with this person?* A good therapist will not take your doubts personally. If you have concerns about what you are hearing the therapist say or discomfort in what you are experiencing, push yourself to ask the therapist questions. Your goal is to determine if you want to hire this person to assist you in your change process.

The therapist should create a safe environment, and in order to do that, she first has to take an "emotional temperature" of sorts. One difference between talking to a friend and talking to a skilled professional is that the latter's job is to keep you grounded as you address your issues. If telling your story gets you wound up before the session is really underway, the therapist may need to begin with some basic grounding exercises to help you relax. Try not to be disappointed if there is not time for your story in the first session. Your therapist must ensure emotional safety first.

A note about couples' intakes

During a couple's intake, it's often the case that one person wants me to hear her story so I'll take her side, and the other wants me to hear his, so I'll take his side. I have to remind them I am not going to take sides. I am there to support their process. My job is not to find fault or point fingers. It is to help clients cope with issues and teach them strategies so they can more effectively cope on their own and with each other. *I know I've done my job when clients no longer need me, and that's what any good therapist should be working toward.*

A final reminder: The therapist is there to help you, not judge you. If you feel you are being judged, find a different therapist. If you continue to meet one judgmental therapist after another, open yourself up to the possibility that your script is projecting judgment when it's not really there. It could be that you are judging yourself, and attributing that judgment to the person who is there to help.

EXERCISE:
SEE THROUGH YOUR SCRIPT WITH MEDITATION

We have addressed the scripts we carry and how they interfere with our ability to see what is real. The following meditation exercise may help you get beyond your script-driven experience toward the wisdom you carry subconsciously, beyond your awareness.

Sit comfortably and quietly. Take a few deep breaths, close your eyes and imagine you are in a beautiful place in nature — a lake, mountain, or beach. With each breath, allow your muscles to let go. Use all of your senses to put yourself in this scene. What can you see in all directions around you? What can you smell? Are there any sounds? If you're on a beach, dig your toes in the sand and feel the water as it laps up over your feet. If you're in a field or glen, smell the wild flowers, or reach out and touch the tall grass. Tilt your face up to the sun and feel the warmth. Breathe. Now, in your mind's eye, see your partner there with you. Don't edit the images that enter your mind, but rather, sit with them and think about what they mean. Are you able to maintain a state of peace in the presence of your partner, or are you seeing something you want to change? Did your partner show up intoxicated, angry, pouting, or with someone else? However your partner showed up, is this a person you want to build a life with? Is this a person you want to parent your children? Is this a person who makes you laugh? Is this a person you can count on when the chips are down?

The purpose of this exercise is to gain access to what your subconscious mind knows about your partner that you might not want to face. Maybe you realize your partner drinks too much, but you have an underlying script that *husbands don't drink too much;* therefore, when you're married, *he won't drink too much.* Maybe you've caught your fiancé lying to you, but your script reads that *wives are honest with husbands,* so once she's your wife *she will be honest.*

This meditation, like all your thoughts and insights, can come from a place of peace and centeredness, and would then likely be a genuine tapping of your intuition. On the other hand, it could be your own intrapersonal *truthiness*,[5] rooted in fear or ego, and as such the information extrapolated reflects more about you and your issues than those of your partner. Only you will know the difference. If you're struggling to figure out what is yours and what belongs to your partner, working with a good therapist could help you tease this out. If that is not a practical option for you at this point, you may be wondering what you can do with insights gained from this exercise.

The first thing to do is stay calm. Insight, no matter how mind-blowing, does not require immediate action or confrontation. You may have a new idea in your head that feels scary or uncomfortable to you. Take whatever time you need to process the new idea before taking action. There are lots of ways to process ideas. You can start a journal or write letters. I recommend doing this the old-fashioned way: pen to paper. You may decide to invite someone else into your process at some point, but at the very start, know that everything you think and write is *all yours*. No one will have access to it without your permission. In fact, write your first draft thinking it will end up in the trash. This will allow you to express your innermost thoughts and feelings without fear of repercussions. Be protective of these ideas; they are private and you want to think carefully before sharing them with anyone. Even if these insights do not lead to a change in your circumstances, they will allow you to approach the relationship with a bit more wisdom.

Whatever you do, stay away from impulsive emails, text messages, and Facebook posts. In our world of fast messaging and connection, it is incredibly important to allow for private processing time and consideration before taking your ideas public.

The goal of the meditation exercise is to help you to see what is real, less colored by your biases, preconceived notions, and expectations. Determining an action plan based on the insights gleaned may take time.

---

[5]Stephen Colbert coined this term in 2005 to reflect the truth we *want* to exist. It's sort of true, based on some of the data available to us. It's *truthy*.

CONCLUSION

Your brain's job is to simplify your world. It creates shortcuts in the form of scripts that help you manage the complexities of life and relationships. We all tend to fit what we see and experience into our scripts and ignore information that doesn't fit. This can create big problems for our relationships if we go into them carrying the assumptions of our scripts and failing to accept our partner *as is*. Our belief that marriage will change whatever is "wrong" with our partners sets us up for failure. Our challenge is to figure out the ways in which our scripts cloud our perception of reality and create self-fulfilling prophecies.

Your first task is to examine your scripts for accuracy. Challenge yourself to see what is real in yourself, your partner, and your relationship. Ask yourself, *"Is this what I expected from myself, from you, and from us?"* The meditation exercise offers one form of visual imagery that might help you to gain insight or have a new idea. Equipped with this new knowledge, you may decide to seek help from a professional to work through the resulting issues. This chapter offered some script-building information about how to find a therapist and what to expect at your first appointment. With a therapist or a trusted confidant, hopefully you will be empowered to edit the scripts that no longer serve you and make the most of the realities in your life.

Marriage provides new opportunities for personal growth and development, but you cannot enter into a marriage *counting on* your partner to change. Over a lifetime together, you will both change and grow — hopefully together and in the same direction. Be that as it may, you cannot count on marriage to fix whatever is wrong with your partner.

MYTH 3:
IF HE WOULD BE PERFECT,
I WOULD BE HAPPY

Asserting *if he (or she) would be perfect, I would be happy*, reveals a need for your partner to provide your happiness. At its core, this myth identifies a tendency to be *dependent* on others. How dependent are you? Complete the four sentences below to find out. Choose *A* or *B*, or write your own response next to option *C*.

```
                    Dependency Quiz
1. When I am hungry, I
        A. want someone to bring me food.
        B. am happy to get my own food.
        C. _____

2. When I am bored, I
        A. want someone to entertain me.
        B. can find something to do for myself.
        C. _____

3. When I am sad, I
        A. want someone to cheer me up.
        B. can cheer myself up.
        C. _____

4. When I am lonely, I
        A. need relief from someone else.
        B. can take care of myself.
        C. _____
```

Completing each sentence with answer *A* reflects dependency, and too much dependency will drag your relationship down. Completing each sentence with answer *B* reflects independence, but too much independence may indicate a disconnection from your partner. Consider a position that combines both options.

> *When I am bored, I want someone to entertain me,*
> **but** *I can find something to do for myself.*

This is a very important **but**, as it addresses our ability to be in balance between *de*pendence and *inde*pendence. *Yes, I would* **prefer** *to be cheered up by my loved one,* **but** *if he isn't available, I* **can** *soothe myself.* I have clients who agree that this is clearly the best approach and describes them. Yet, when confronted with evidence of their own dependency or neediness, they protest. I recall one wife who declared:

> *"Of course I don't expect him to be perfect! He doesn't have to be perfect. He just needs to be there when I need him, doing what I need him to be doing, the way I want him to be doing it."*

If that isn't expecting perfection, I don't know what is.

If you find yourself complaining about your spouse, starting sentences with *I need him to ...*, perhaps you are overly dependent on your spouse to provide for your needs. That would place an undue burden on him (or her) to be perfect in the relationship and reveal your own neediness. You might be under the spell of this myth.

The consequences of this myth vary widely. Let's say you are operating under the belief that you would be happy if your partner were "perfect." You might find that you move from one relationship to another looking for the "perfect" match and unable to get your needs met. If you examine that more closely, you might discover a tendency to turn your needs into your partner's flaws. This can lead to a break-up and is usually at work when someone experiences multiple divorces. However, this myth can also keep an otherwise reasonable person stuck in an unfulfilling relationship long past its natural expiration date. Think about it: If we-as-a-couple are unhappy because *you* are not meeting *my* needs, then:

(1) I am under no obligation to take ownership of any part of our difficulties;
(2) If I nag, cajole, or otherwise harass you sufficiently, I'll get you to change — to adopt the behaviors that will make me happy; and
(3) I don't have to change my behavior or myself.

In short, this myth keeps you stuck in your perspective by validating and verifying your position as the victim. You can either walk away feeling totally justified, or you can stay "victim" in your marriage.

As *neediness* is the personal quality at the core of this myth, let's look at a case example of a woman unable to cope with these feelings. She turned her needs into her husband's flaws.

Ben, Nadine, and the Honey-Do P-List

Ben was a traveling salesman from St. Louis. His business took him to New York four nights each week. When his wife, Nadine, found a "gentlemen's magazine" in his bag after one of his trips, she flew into a rage and demanded he find a therapist to address his sex addiction. Over the next several weeks, Nadine developed a list of all his faults he would need to address in order to save the marriage. The list covered a range of personal and interpersonal items. First, he needed to be a better husband and more tuned into her needs as a wife and mother. Second, he needed to be more active in disciplining the children, and less nosy about how she spent money. Next, he needed to cut out his boys' nights, in fact, no more drinking during the week. Finally, he needed to lose a few pounds because he was starting to look old and out of shape. Nadine sent Ben in for counseling to address these imperfections. She wanted nothing to do with the process.

The "honey-do list" is a fairly well known marital construct. It's a list a wife provides to her husband that itemizes household chores (e.g., change light bulbs, tighten door hinges, open stuck windows). In marital therapy, I keep an ear out for the dreaded *Honey-Do P-List*, which includes items in need of fixing from any of six main areas: Partnering, Parenting, Providing, Partying, Power, and Personal hygiene.

In Ben's case, his therapy goals were clear. He needed to address his Honey-Do P-List and become the *Mary Poppins* of husbands — *practically perfect in every way*. His first session proceeded the way most do for husbands in this position. He began by profusely committing to address his flaws so that he could meet Nadine's needs and save his marriage. After a few weeks, he offered plenty of examples of improvement, such as doing more around the house, staying home on weeknights, and working out. Problem solved, and we're ready to terminate our counseling sessions, right? It's never this simple. Nadine *still* felt tremendously disconnected from Ben, which did not come as a surprise to me, because:

The discontent that inspires a Honey-Do P-List cannot be repaired by superficial gestures.

Ben's behavior is now practically perfect, and yet, she's still not satisfied. Her continued discontent leads to a sense of frustration on his part and a painful realization on hers: *I just don't love him anymore*. She might be ready for this insight, in which case, the transition out of the marriage can be sad but amicable. If she cannot admit to herself that she wants out of the marriage, she may act out with infidelity or find new things to nag about, subconsciously driving him away so that it will be *his* choice to end the marriage, not hers.

Fault-finding and then blaming marital problems on your spouse's imperfections is not new, nor is it particularly complicated. It's another example of what can result if you are not open to or honest about what's incomplete or hurting within your *self,* and it's often expressed in the form of *"not getting my needs met."* After all, it feels safer to point to your partner's failure to meet your needs than to dig into your neediness and the deeper issues your neediness may reveal. So let's look at that a bit more closely.

THE BIG FOUR

When we have feelings we cannot admit to having, they prompt us to use *defenses* to protect our *selves*. Some of these aversive feelings I encounter so often with clients, I refer to them as The Big Four: **Fear, Shame, Guilt,** and **Ego.** It doesn't feel good to feel shame, so we defend ourselves against that feeling of *shame*. It doesn't feel good to feel guilt, so we defend ourselves against our own *guilt*. Often times, our way of defending ourselves against these difficult feelings is to throw blame out to those around us.

***If you divorce me, then I don't have to feel bad
about my true desire to leave the marriage.***

For Nadine, any or all of The Big Four could be at work. Let's look at each of them and see what might be going on.

FEAR
Nadine may be afraid to end the marriage. What could she fear? Put yourself in Nadine's shoes, close your eyes, and think about this for a moment before reading on.

Did you come up with any of these?

- *What will my family (especially my children) and friends think?*
- *How would I survive the economic hit?*
- *Will he turn on me during the divorce?*
- *What if I end up old and alone?*

Appreciate the fact that fear is a future-oriented emotion. You cannot be *afraid* of what's in the past. Memories can certainly evoke strong emotions, but *fear* itself must be about something yet to be, either pending or possible. Nadine could be afraid of what the reality of life after divorce might be, and with good reason. Research indicates women and their children are much more likely than men to be socio-economically downgraded after a divorce. There is reason to fear being a single parent. At every stage of your children's development, single-parenthood presents extreme challenges.

Nadine's fear could relate much more to the basic human need for companionship. The fear of *ending up alone* is a powerful force. It relates to fears about the aging process, the mourning of youth, even the fear of death itself. Nadine has an extra layer of anxiety over this because, as a practicing Christian, she believes she is not *supposed to* fear death.

Nadine's fear may be preventing her from taking ownership of her desire to leave the marriage. Instead, she may act out in ways that drive her husband to leave *her*.

SHAME

In order to explore *shame,* it is helpful to understand the "inner parts" of the human experience. We have an impulsive and needy part that wants to feel good all the time, we have a judgmental part that beats us up for having that needy part, and we have a part in the middle helping us live in the real world by working to satisfy the other two. Freud called them the id, superego, and ego, respectively; Transactional Analysis (TA) asserts they are all parts of the ego-state and calls them the child, parent, and adult. I use the terms interchangeably, and the bottom line is this: We each have a critical parent/superego that "shoulds" on us. *"You should be doing this. You shouldn't be doing that!"* This inner, critical voice is the source of *shame.*

Sit quietly for a moment and listen to this critical, inner voice. You may recognize it, as it often sounds like the voice of a parent or oppressive teacher from your past. Every so often, my old driver's ed teacher will join me in a traffic situation. I can't recall his name, but I can see his face and hear his voice when I hustle through an intersection when the light is yellow. *(I **shouldn't** have done that!)* In this case, *shame* is a helpful feeling, because next time I will drive more carefully.

Shame is interesting because it is not tied to a tangible consequence; rather, it is the feeling we experience in response to what we've done, thought, or said that an inner voice judges to be immoral. *"SHAME on you,"* scolds this inner, critical parent whenever your behavior or thought strays outside the boundaries of "good" behavior.

Shame is a conditioned feeling.

Let's be honest; most major religions use *shame* as a tool for compliance. The church police couldn't possibly be everywhere at once, so what better way to get large numbers of people to comply with their rules? Install inner-thought cams inside every member of the congregation, always watching, always judging. *No need to police those who have been conditioned to police themselves.*

I remember as a kid being fascinated by the idea that God was everywhere and always watching. It didn't really bother me because He never seemed to take action no matter what my behavior; plus, I always had this sense that He wasn't nearly as judgmental as adults would have me believe. I was pretty sure He would have been on my side most of the time, anyway. I was more concerned with Santa's elves, who, according to my mother, were also watching all the time and eager to rat me out to Santa (the little tattle-tales). I can remember looking sideways towards the picture window in our kitchen, wanting to catch one of those little bastards peeking in, list in hand trying to get the goods on me.

Now that I am a grown up and a parent, I *get* that adults need to install moral compasses in their young, so they might grow up to perpetuate the cultural values. (My own children are now on the lookout for those elves.) On one hand, it's all very sociologically compelling and arguably necessary for cultural survival. However, whatever good it does for the society, it can do a number on the individual members. Children raised in extremely shaming environments can have tremendous difficulty as adults, ruled by the domineering superego, unable to live authentically in their own skin.

I see clients riddled with anxiety who suffer terribly because they were taught to be ashamed of themselves and their bodies.

Parenting in the past twenty years has changed, shifting from shame-based, *"You are a bad girl,"* to focus instead on behavior, *"You are wonderful, but your behavior is unacceptable!"* This separation of *self* from *behavior* is yielding a new crop of young adults, and the verdict is still out as to how much of an improvement this is for the society as a whole or for the individual members. There is a growing sense of entitlement that comes with a healthy sense of self, and that entitlement has an upside (they know their worth and will not accept anything less) and a downside (they may feel deserving of rewards and recognition for less-than-exceptional behavior). Perhaps it's worth noting the difference between shame and humility. *Humility* means to have modesty of self-opinion. Maybe in our collective effort to ditch shame-based parenting, we've unwittingly thrown out humility, too. In the absence of humility, what emerges is arrogance, which is exceedingly destructive to human relationships. We will talk more about arrogance and humility in Chapter 4.

What makes *shame* such a unique construct is that the judge, jury, and jailor are all inside your head. Maybe I conclude, *"I shouldn't have done that,"* but what metric did I use to determine my behavior was *bad?* Is the standard I used truly coming from within me, or is it someone else's moral judgment I've been conditioned to accept as my own? Stop for a moment and see if you can come up with an example of a behavior that causes you to feel *ashamed*. After you come up with an example, think about *why* you feel shame. Perhaps what comes to you sounds like the following:

"If my mother knew, she'd be ashamed of me, so I am ashamed of myself."

Although it may be true that your mother would be ashamed of you if she found out, do you *agree* with her judgment that the behavior was shameful? If so, then it is a good time to explore the resulting *shame* as a helpful feeling, intended to assist you to shape your behavior towards expressing your best *self*. If not, if you don't agree that your behavior was inherently shameful, then your shame is a conditioned response, and not really aligned with who you are in the here and now. The conditioned *shame* may have outlasted its usefulness.

Let's connect this to Nadine. She was married to a good man who treated her well, provided a nice lifestyle for their family, and deserved to be loved. Perhaps wanting out of such a marriage was simply not acceptable to her family, church, or community. More importantly, it may be her own critical inner-voice, berating her for feeling such discontent, resulting in her shame. If her superego is *shoulding* on her for wanting out of a *"good"* marriage, we can safely assume *shame* is keeping her stuck and driving the criticism of her husband.

GUILT

What role might guilt play for Nadine, and how might it be related to shame? As a construct, guilt differs from shame in that while shame is really all about the *self,* guilt is very specifically tied to a projected or actual consequence that touches others.

> ***Once the affair was revealed, she felt ashamed of what she had done, and she felt guilty about the impact it would have on her husband and children.***

Guilt and shame are closely related and sometimes entangled ideas. Let's look at a concrete example before getting back to the role guilt might be playing for Nadine.

> *Susan, a married woman with three young children, met Alex during Circle Time at the local library. After flirting for months, the two began an affair. While having the affair, she felt both ashamed because she knew she was committing a sin and guilty about what it might do to her family if discovered. She felt particularly shameful for using her children as cover, and guilty about not confiding in her best girlfriend.*

All of these feelings are real, but Susan might not take time to unpack them. She could develop anxiety or depression, or she could live day to day completely unaware of these inner feelings. After all, her id is in *hog heaven!* She feels like a teenager again, free to sneak around and rekindle a sexuality so long gone it had been all but forgotten. When the superego and id are in such deep conflict, the ego steps in to make it all work. She could justify her need for a lover because her husband is so neglectful, she's so lonely, or she's made so many sacrifices to take the role of wife and mother that she deserves a little fun. She could deny there's any conflict at all, instead believing her husband deserves it and the kids will never know. However, the guilt is in there somewhere, buried beneath these defenses.

For Nadine, guilt could have been preventing her from leaving her marriage. It certainly seems like the thought of tearing her family apart and what that would mean for her children's wellbeing would overwhelm her with guilt. She had seen children of divorced parents shuttled back-and-forth between homes throughout the week and every other weekend. She could not imagine putting her own children on such a schedule, shattering the sense of family unity she and Ben had created. She tried to picture breaking the news to her children, but visualizing the heartbreak in their eyes stopped her cold. It is very possible she felt their pain so viscerally she simply could not initiate that grief in their lives. Guilt could be keeping her stuck.

EGO

We have talked about *ego* as one of Freud's three inner parts of the *self*. Most of us don't think of *ego* in this way. To most people, it means arrogance and vanity. *"What an EGO on that guy!"* is usually understood to mean he is *egotistical,* full of himself. It's connected to a strong self-concept, high self-esteem, and abundant pride. We think of people with too much ego as aloof and self-centered; not enough, and they are mousy and weak. Yet, that's taking the ego out of context. The ego is just doing its job as described earlier — helping to get the needs of the id met under the watchful and judgmental eye of the superego.

Take, as an example, admitting mistakes. When someone makes a mistake and won't admit it, the easy explanation is that she's too proud, and she has *too much ego*. Flip that, and see it from the perspective of her inner parts. If she has a particularly abusive superego, she is going to work very hard to please it. Like a five-year-old child stammering to explain how her painted handprint ended up on the lampshade, her inner child stands in judgment before her critical parent. The greater her need to be right all the time actually tells us how much bullying she gets from her superego. This understanding may inspire more compassion for and understanding of her choices and actions.

This inner conflict could be in play for Nadine. Her id (or inner child) no longer feels good in the marriage. She wants out. Her superego cannot believe she wants out of a perfectly good marriage, and is *shoulding* on her because she *shouldn't* feel that way. This leaves her ego with the task of trying to help the id feel better while appeasing the superego. Her ego is simply trying to cope. If Ben were a lousy husband, she could leave the marriage without incurring the wrath of the superego, hence her fault-finding.

IN DEFENSE OF DEFENSIVENESS

So far, I have highlighted how we defend against The Big Four, but I need to be clear: You cannot live without them, either. In moderation,

- *Fear keeps us safe.*
- *Shame keeps us humble.*
- *Guilt keeps us from hurting others.*
- *Ego allows us to survive in the world.*

Still, when any of The Big Four slips into the driver's seat without your acknowledgment, awareness, or permission, issues will arise. You will react *defensively* when there is not an actual threat pending. Fear, shame, guilt, and ego swirl through our daily lives and create the underlying motivation for behavior. We can understand the way we act, react, and occasionally *overreact* by exploring these aspects of our *selves*. Each in its own way, collectively they help us to avoid what is painful, what feels unsafe, and in some cases, what is really going on.

Regardless of the underlying motivation for Nadine, the consequence is true avoidance of ownership and responsibility. Until she takes ownership of her own experiences and feelings, she cannot begin the work of rebuilding her marriage, nor can she move towards divorce. She will remain stuck.

Unfortunately for Ben, Nadine refused to come in for help. She remained insistent that Ben simply could not meet her needs. As long as it was his shortcomings causing her unhappiness, her own neediness was irrelevant. It was too much for her to admit she wanted out of the marriage. Whether the underlying cause of her neediness was her fear, shame, guilt, or ego, she divorced Ben under the pretense that he had been too big a failure as a husband. In the years after the divorce, it was revealed that she had been dating someone during their marriage. Betrayal in a marriage is heartbreaking, but for her as the betrayer to justify her behavior and blame it on the betrayed? That's the crazy making that adds insult to injury. *"If he could have been more (fill in the blank), then I wouldn't have needed to (fill in the blank)."* We hear this from deeply unhappy people operating under the Big Four and working hard to justify their actions.

CONCLUSION: LIVING YOUR SPIRIT

Some people wonder, *if you take away my fear, shame, guilt, and ego, what's left of me?* With The Big Four appropriately positioned out of the driver's seat and (hopefully) towards the back of the bus, what's left is the best part: *Your Spirit,* your truest inner self.

It is my sincere hope that you can think of lots of examples of when you personally are in your spirit. For some, it's sitting on a beach, watching a sunset, or swaying gently while holding a sleeping baby. For others, it's creating art, dancing, or playing an instrument. You know you are in spirit when nothing else matters in that moment. It's pure. Time seems to stop. No fear, shame, guilt, or ego. All is right in your world.[6]

When you live your spirit, it becomes easy to recognize the spirit in others. When you see another's spirit, it is much easier to look past all of the earthly concerns that bind up a relationship. Our earthly stuff (fear, shame, guilt, and ego) often prevents us from living our spirit and seeing spirit in others. In Chapter 8, we will look at the perils and pitfalls of perfection in depth, but for now, if you are looking to your spouse to change, *to become perfect,* in order to ensure your happiness, it is doubtful that you are walking your own best, spiritual path.

---

[6]If you want to read more about living your spirit, I recommend you become acquainted with the work of Sonia Choquette. She offers books, seminars, and a host of other resources to support this process.

MYTH 4:
LET'S MAKE A DEAL:
THE BARTER ECONOMY MARRIAGE

Give and take is a natural part of most relationships, and marriage is no exception. In fact, most marriages operate under this myth to some degree. You trade your goods and services for a return. *"I'll do this for you, and you'll do this for me."* People who believe such a bargain *guarantees* happily ever after have surrendered to this myth. A breech of their agreement is often what prompts couples to seek help. Let's say she was upholding her end of the bargain and discovers he was not. Feeling like the wronged party, she drags him in for therapy, but while engaged in the work, he reveals the ways in which *her* breeches led to his breeches. *Breeches* can be anything from, *"I can't get him to take out the trash"* to *"He's having an affair." "She won't leave me alone at work"* to *"She's been stashing away money behind my back."*

When couples seek help, a successful reconciliation depends on the severity of the breeches, their willingness to forgive each other, their motivation to strike a new agreement, and their ability to trust they are entering the new bargain in good faith. This can be a monumental, even insurmountable challenge, especially in the aftermath of a betrayal.

Each person in the relationship can be operating under his or her own assumed barter agreement, or the couple may strike deals with each other as they go. A common agreement is, *"I'll make the money, and you'll take care of the home and kids."* Let's face it; this oversimplified division of labor minimizes the tremendous effort and skills it takes to make a family work.

RUNNING THE FAMILY BUSINESS

The family is like a business. It needs an accounting department to attend to budgeting, create spending allowances, keep the books, pay the bills, and establish savings for a variety of purposes — retirement, education, weddings, overnight camp. The Family Business also needs a housekeeping staff to address a variety of cleaning chores on a daily basis, like washing dishes, and weekly ones, like laundry and bathrooms, and finally, seasonal tasks, like windows and closets. And the clutter! Every Family Business could use a professional organizer to address the basic flow of *stuff*. So much comes in via the mail, backpacks, and shopping as a normal part of the day, but there is no such natural flow *outward,* except for the trashiest of trash that ends up in the garbage can. It can feel like a full-time job just to address issues of clutter around the home. A maintenance crew is required for the inside of the home, attending to air filters, light fixtures, home mechanics, and the like, while the grounds crew attends to the lawn, garden, gutters, shutters, roof, shrubs, and dog poo.

The Family Business could also use a tutor for the children, a therapist to address their developmental needs and marital issues as they arise, and a social planner to handle birthday parties, holidays, and vacations. The kitchen staff would include a meal planner, shopper, and of course, a chef.

Families do their best to allocate *all* of these responsibilities to its members in a way that works for them. Some have a clear "outside/inside" division, so one partner attends to outside matters, earning money from another business and tending to the yard, home exterior, and cars, while the other tends to everything inside the home, including the children. Some families divide it cross-sectionally, with both adults generating income and both contributing to the care of the children and home. Rarely is the division 50/50, but it ebbs and flows over time with the needs of the family and professional opportunities of the adults. And of course, it is appropriate to get the kids helping

around the house and yard early on, doing age-appropriate tasks. Once the crew gets involved, our Family Business needs a personnel director and supervisor on top of everything else.

> ***What am I doing to make it work, what are you doing to make it work, and is it an equitable, if not even, trade?***

In short, is it fair? The barter system can work quite well when there is very strong communication and clear understanding of who's doing what and when, and towards what end. Such clarity is not always the case, and clarity alone does not always mean an equitable or comfortable division of labor.

Harriet and Edward: A Lopsided Agreement
Harriet came into my office on a scouting mission. She wanted some individual work, but she really wanted to find someone for her husband, Edward. Because he was so brilliant, it would be difficult to find a therapist he would find acceptable. Edward suffered from a condition I call academentia, *a distorted way of experiencing the world based on extended time and immersion in an academic environment. One symptom of academentia is the erroneous belief that because you are learned in one area, you have exceptional competence or intelligence in other areas as well. Her husband was under the false belief that his brilliance transcended his business management and applied to all aspects of his life, including his personal life and relationships. No one would know more than he knew.*

Harriet was unhappy in her marriage and tired of being taken for granted, and Edward knew nothing of her discontent. They met when she was a brilliant and beautiful young businesswoman in her first job post-MBA, and he was a promising vice president in the company. The chemistry was undeniable, and within a year, they were married. She quit her job two years later, when the first of their three children was born. When the youngest was in preschool, Harriet started a home-based business, coordinating assisted living services to seniors. Just as the business was taking off, Edward had an opportunity to advance his career, which required relocating. She sold her business and followed him to another state, and a few years later to another, and then another. Financially, the moves were very good, but in every other way, they were terrible. The children were constantly changing schools and starting over. Just when Harriet would develop some friends and roots in a community, it was time to go again. And with each move, she worked tirelessly to set up a new home, transition the children to the new community, and play hostess to his new work colleagues and subordinates.

Edward's job took him around the world to places Harriet would have loved to go, but she rarely joined him. Sometimes the children had things going on she couldn't miss. Sometimes the trip wasn't open to spouses. Harriet loved to travel and Edward promised it would be her turn some day. The excuses changed over time. Early on, it was "when his career was really sailing." After his career had, by all measures, leveled off at the top, it was "when the business trips allow for more fun and leisure time." Recently, it was "when he's retired, and they can just go on fun trips without business obligations." As the years went by, his career continued to flourish, she never did get a chance to travel, start another business, or do anything except take care of the children and the house. Although they had money to hire full-time help in and around the home, she felt pressured to personally attend to every last detail, and oversee even the smallest of jobs. She was strong-willed and athletic but became a nervous wreck when Edward was en route home, wanting to make everything perfect for him.

Harriet and Edward had a deal. He earned money and prestige and in exchange, he wanted an impeccably clean house and tidy yard, food in the refrigerator, clean laundry pressed and put away, a full tank of gas in the car, good sex, and happy children. All of this she did, and in exchange she wanted ... well, that's part of the problem. She didn't know what she wanted. In their youth, she had wanted to be his partner, but she settled for playing the supporting role, professionally and personally. After a few years of marriage, she became invisible to him, like any other subordinate in any one of his companies. She settled into a marriage that felt more like a job, but one day she would get her reward. He would retire and they would travel around the world as partners!

Her awakening came upon his return from an extended overseas trip. She'd picked him up in their car (which had a full tank of gas), brought him home to a clean house where they dined on a lovely meal *she'd prepared, he changed into casual clothes that had been laundered and neatly folded in his drawer, just where he expected them to be. A pleasant evening passed, capped with comfortable if not passionate sex. As they prepared for sleep, she said, "I can't wait until we are off somewhere exotic in the world, just the two of us." It seemed in reach, now that their youngest daughter was finishing college. He sighed, and expressed doubts. "I think I've just about had it with traveling. I'm looking forward to just staying put once I'm retired."*

*And there it was. The latest in a string of pronouncements, like so many before, declaring what was to be for them. She'd paid her dues, made her sacrifices, given up so much of her own ambitions for him and for this marriage, and now here in this moment, it was infinitely clear to her there would never be the payoff she expected, or more accurately, **earned**.*

Many women live their lives for the promise of "some day." As children, we dream along with Snow White, *"Someday my prince will come."* As teenagers, we hold the promise of independence once we leave our parents' homes. We transition into adulthood with the expectation that we will be happy when … This is when it gets a bit tricky. When what? Land the perfect job or the perfect man? Get married and have children? It's easy for women to continue the cycle of thinking when a man offers that option, as Harriet had done. Men can also be disillusioned in adulthood if they learn that working hard does not guarantee success, and success does not guarantee happiness. Even success and happiness do not guarantee *happily ever after* if you disenfranchise your life partner along the way, as Edward had.

Although many partners in a "tit-for-tat" arrangement like Harriet and Edward's live under unspoken assumptions about their deal, the barter economy marriage can end in heartache if one person counts on it but the other thinks, *"Sure, it is possible."* There is a world of difference between a plan and a possibility. Because the human brain is wired to hear what it wants to hear, our spouse saying, "maybe" can be heard as "likely" or even "yes" if we want it badly enough.

Harriet embarked on a roller coaster of emotions that included anger over their broken deal and utter sadness for the choices she'd made. She was seen by peers as the privileged wife of a wealthy man, but she was invisible in her own home. And her beautiful daughters! What kind of example had she set for them? How could they respect a woman who had sacrificed her *self* for a man? Although her sadness was palpable, she did not feel self-pity; she was angry with herself. *"Poor little rich girl,"* she seethed. All of this pain was necessary as she shook off her old skin. In addition, like all great awakenings of the human spirit, her transition included some denial, bargaining, anger, and depression, and eventually what emerged was acceptance.[7] Her journey to live her true spirit had begun.

When families have the luxury[8] of living on a single income, more typically the woman sacrifices her professional ambitions while the man sacrifices personal interests and parenting time for the family, although that picture is changing. The first decade of the 21st century is over, more families are sending into the workforce whoever has the greater earning potential, and the result is an increase in dads taking on the role of primary care provider, working a schedule around the children. As the economic gluttony of the late 20th and early 21st centuries yields to a market correction that requires a paring down of credit and spending across the entire system, working families are caught in the shift. Many couples who shared a vision of happily as well as *comfortably* ever after are seeing their dreams vanish as retirement funds and pensions disappear, or medical bills gobble up savings and drive bankruptcy.[9] This is a major breech of the agreement for the traditional family *providers*. They've missed ball games and recitals. They settled for long weekends instead of weeklong vacations. They spent the formative years of their children's lives in pursuit of an economic security that blew up.

---

[7]These are the stages of grief offered by Elisabeth Kübler-Ross. We will address them in more detail in Chapter 6.

[8]Lest the word *luxury* confuse anyone, I don't mean they are necessarily living a luxurious lifestyle. On the contrary, I know many hard working families that make the choice to sacrifice a second car, vacations, and retirement funds in order to enable one parent to stay at home. Still, even with such sacrifices, not everyone can make it on a single income, even when they forego the aforementioned "luxury" items.

[9]According to multiple sources, about half of bankruptcy filings are the direct or indirect result of medical expenses, even though 75% of those who filed had health insurance.

We will pick up the topic of *shared sacrifice for tomorrow's payoff* in the next chapter. For now, let's get back to Harriet and Edward. She traded her life in exchange for a future she clearly wasn't going to have, not because of an economic crisis in her family, but because her husband wasn't going to hold up his end of the bargain.

INFIDELITY: THE ULITMATE DEAL-BREAKER

Like every barter exchange, there are conditions that go along with the deal. Consider this inner-monologue of a woman who has taken a traditional role in her marriage:

"I'll stay home and tend to the family's needs, and while you're out in the world to support us you'll be faithful to me and our marriage."

This is an assumption she makes and a bargain her husband is eager to enter. *Of course* he will be faithful! What happens when he's not? Usually, nothing ... until he gets caught. I have yet to meet the husband who confesses to an ongoing affair because he is riddled with guilt or shame, afraid of being caught or of what might happen to his family if he is caught. That's not to say only men cheat. Sadly, husbands *and* wives cheat; however, it is my observation that men and women cheat for different reasons with different outcomes. Women are more likely to cheat because they are unhappy in the marriage and looking for a way out. Men are more likely to cheat for the instant gratification, without intention of disrupting their home or family. Yes, there are exceptions, and of course, the gender differences are narrowing as old roles and stereotypes change. Keep in mind, *I am only talking about those open to infidelity*. Those who are not are not included here. In my experience, for those open to infidelity, the old expression holds true: Women need an excuse to cheat, while men simply need an opportunity.

Men who have affairs believe they are entitled to step out of the marriage, and they boldly believe the deceit will not be discovered. Ladies, it really isn't personal, even though nothing could be more personally devastating than to discover such a betrayal. In Harriet's case, an angry ex-girlfriend of Edward's called to reveal the truth.

*Kat had been seeing Edward for a number of years, going on trips together, meeting at hotels in the city. She didn't expect Edward would ever leave Harriet, but she did expect Edward would be "faithful" to her, and when she discovered he had another girlfriend, longer term, whom he housed in an upscale condo downtown, Kat flipped. She had accepted her role as the other woman as part of their deal, but to discover she was the **other** other woman was too much for her, and a breech of their bargain.*

As is typical, Edward's affair with Kat was discovered by Harriet, not disclosed by Edward. Edward denied any wrongdoing until Harriet presented evidence to him, and even then, only confessed to the bare minimum. Edward first denied knowing Kat. Then, he admitted she was a business colleague who happened to travel in similar circles. Then it was a "one-time thing" he had regretted immediately. When he couldn't deny the on-going affair, he explained it was only because Kat was crazy; he had to continue seeing her because she was threatening to tell Harriet about his one mistake. On and on the lies went as Edward tried to cling to his profession of innocence ... or at least to a lesser crime than the truth.

The assumption that *you will be faithful to me* is often a non-negotiable part of the marital bargain. Once broken, the original deal cannot be repaired without intense intervention, and even then, it might not be recoverable. *"Who cheated?"* and *"Why?"* are important variables to unpack in the aftermath of such betrayal.

	Unhappy/Cry for help	Bored/For Sport
Wife	She may want to save the marriage but his pride might not allow for that option. Therapy *might* work depending on his ability to forgive, heal, and own his role in her unhappiness.	She will likely find a new husband and leave the marriage. Without intense therapy and personal insight, the pattern will repeat in her next marriage.
Husband	He may want to save the marriage, and she will likely stay to work it out. With commitment and therapy, they have a good prognosis for building a new marriage that suites them both.	He believes his wife will not discover his betrayal and is shocked when she does. He likely wants to keep his family in tact. Without intense therapy and personal insight, the pattern will repeat.

If a wife cheated because she was unhappy, her husband may not be able to forgive her. Even when he can forgive, his pride may prevent him from taking ownership of his role in her unhappiness, which prevents full recovery and ultimately ends the marriage. If a husband cheats because he is unhappy, his wife is more likely to own her role in their marital discord, and so there is a good chance the marriage can be saved with professional assistance. If either (or both) of them cheated for sport, because they were bored or looking for instant gratification, the likelihood of saving the marriage drops considerably. If this is the case, it is possible that the real culprit is *arrogance.*

THE UGLY TRUTH ABOUT ARROGANCE

The ugly truth is that *arrogance,* overbearing pride, inflated self-worth to the point of pathological thinking, is a vice that kills relationships. Maybe that's why it's condemned by so many religions. It's the Christian Bible's Deadly Sin mentioned also in the Book of Proverbs, the Koran, and the Book of Mormon. Why is it considered so evil by so many?

Everyone is born with gifts, and our human directive is to identify our gifts and figure out how they can best serve our communities. You **have** to have a strong sense of self, self-confidence, and a healthy ego to do this. Let's say you have these qualities, figure out your gifts, get your training and credentials in order, and venture out to share your gifts with the world, becoming wildly successful in the process. So far, that sounds like Edward. So what goes wrong? Edward's character is evident in his attributions.

To what does Edward attribute his success?

This is the key question, and his answer reveals his arrogance. He believes he alone is responsible. He has no gratitude for the genes his parents gave him, the environment in which he was raised, the privilege of his world class education, or the countless people in his life: family, teachers, mentors, friends, colleagues, and of course Harriet, each of whom played a role in shaping his experiences and opportunities. He has no humility in knowing that if any of these variables had been different, his journey would have been different too, with perhaps a very different outcome. This arrogant man is like a stubborn two-year-old who pronounces, "I DO IT MY*SELF*."

Like Edward, you cannot have a healthy marriage if you lack a profound sense of gratitude and humility for the gifts in your life. With arrogance comes a sense of entitlement. Under these conditions, your partner will become invisible. You will fail to recognize she is with you by choice, and she could choose not to be. That is a humbling thought, easier to ignore than to process, especially for those with a pathological need for success.

UPDATING THE AGREEMENT

We've explored how marriages operate under a barter system, exchanging goods, services, and loyalty, but also that a bargain is not a guarantee for *Happily Ever After*. Marriage requires attention and care, and it is too easy to get stuck in assumptions based on old deals and grow blind to the here-and-now realities of the relationship. I cannot think of any contractual agreement that goes on in perpetuity. Even marriage is only entered *"until death do us part."* Yet, we expect the deals we make with a new spouse in our twenties to be a lifelong lock. That's just unrealistic. You have to keep your deal up-to-date as life circumstances change and you both evolve. At least once a year, you and your spouse need to set aside time to assess how your agreements are working, how they can be improved, and how they need to be adjusted to suit upcoming changes. I recommend holding an annual meeting to address these issues, and I describe that process in detail in the next chapter.

Give and take is an important process in every relationship. The agreements we make set the stage for success or failure, depending on the balance of give and take, the communication around the agreements, the commitment of each person to the agreements, and finally, the flexibility to adjust agreements over time under changing circumstances. My hope is that this chapter inspires you and your partner to review and assess the agreements you have with each other, so that you each can take ownership of your parts of the agreements, and approach one another with mindfulness and love as you work to create a balanced partnership in the years ahead.

LESSONS FROM A BOILING FROG

If you put a frog in boiling water, he will jump out and save himself. If you put that same frog in tepid water, you can gradually turn up the heat until he boils to death. Why doesn't the frog save himself? Because he adapts to the water as it gets hotter and hotter. Humans are like this, too. We start with a reasonable slate of responsibilities and commitments, and then we take on more and more until our schedule is completely overwhelming, but we've adapted to each addition, not realizing we've put ourselves in jeopardy. We rarely pause long enough to take an inventory of all that we do.

Your challenge is to hop out of your pot and find out how rapidly your water is boiling. Keep a journal for a week that details all that you do for everyone in your life. Below is an example of a table with columns to help organize this information.

To-Do Item	Why do it?	Cost/Benefits	Was it appreciated?	How am I feeling about it?	How can I make it easier?
make lunches	have to	save $$, healthier than cafeteria or fast food	no	Fine, no bother	Pack lunch in p.m. Get Bob to help.
do the laundry	have to	clean laundry	no	Irritated. Found clean shirt in dirty basket.	Kids could help, esp. putting away
lunch volunteer	want to	get to see the kids, the school needs the help	a bit	Good. I like seeing other moms, too.	cut back to 1x per week
work at pet shop	have to	we need the money, but the boss is a creep and hard work conditions	yes	Burdened. I hate going.	find a new job

I have no doubt you could fill pages with all that you do daily and weekly for your family and community. If it feels like you are stretched thin, this exercise might help you to understand why. At the end of the week, take a look at the connections between what you did and how you felt. Use your journal to make some executive decisions about dividing responsibilities more equitably in the home, balancing joyful activities with those that feel like "work," and upping the expectations for gratitude among the beneficiaries of your hard work. Laying it all out like this might also help you quickly identify the most troublesome parts of your schedule. In the above example, this person might do well to focus on changing her job situation, as that seems to stand out as an exceptionally unpleasant activity for her.

CONCLUSION

Relationships involve give and take, and compromise often includes accounting for what the exchange will involve. *"I'll do this for you, and in exchange you'll do this for me."* Each enters the deal trying to maximize personal happiness and ensure the ongoing relationship. It takes a tremendous effort to run a family, and because the demands change quickly as children grow and circumstances change, it is important for couples to communicate effectively about their agreements. Couples reach the most effective compromises when both are willing to sacrifice a little happiness for the sake of the relationship. If the sacrifices are not balanced, if one person is sacrificing much more than the other, there will likely be breeches in the agreement that require professional help.

Couples should spell out the terms of their agreement early and revisit them often so that one person does not wake up one day and find he or she was investing in a one-sided deal. I recommend both partners create tables like the example in this chapter, itemizing all that they do, so they can come together and share in each other's joys and burdens, renegotiate deals that no longer serve them, and see the specific areas in which they need to be more helpful to one another and appreciative of each other's efforts.

MYTH 5:
WE'LL BE HAPPY WHEN WE GET THERE

In Barter Economy Marriages, spouses make agreements about what they will do for each other. *"We'll Be Happy When We Get There"* is about what they will do together for a better tomorrow. Whether their agreements are expressly shared with one another (overt) or quietly influencing from beyond awareness (covert), they are hard to crack because two partners can be completely united in a delusion that "happy" is some place out in the future, and it's okay merely to *survive* the present.

**This myth is in play when the couple shares
the sacrifices today for a better tomorrow.**

At its worst, misery loves company in this marriage, and discord and discomfort are tolerated because of the shared belief that better times are ahead. We will look at an example in which the sacrifices weighed heavily on the children later in this chapter. At best, these marriages survive on an even keel with no major ups or downs, and the couples do not dwell on their shared sacrifices. In fact, the sacrifices they make may seem pretty mild to some: foregoing fancy cars for their children's college funds or skipping extravagant vacations to contribute to retirement. These are questions of choice, not survival.

We'll start with a case painfully close to many Americans — those who scrimped and saved for retirement only to see their life savings disappear during the financial crisis of 2008.

Barry and Tina: An American Dream Goes Bust

Barry worked hard as an engineer for a local manufacturing company. He enjoyed his job for the first ten years, but got bored with it about the same time his family needed the most financial support; young mouths and college savings accounts all needed regular feeding. He went to work; he was paid. His satisfaction came from his paycheck, not the job. After twenty-six years, the children had graduated, and he had about fifteen years left until retirement. He decided to gut it out until then. After all, it had never been about his job satisfaction. His priority was his family. He and his wife, Tina, could certainly look back on the American Dream their life had been! They raised three children in the same town in which they'd grown up, watched them graduate from the same high school, attend the same summer camps, and get married in the same church they had attended for every holiday, baptism, wedding, and funeral. Tina had worked part-time at a local florist shop since their youngest started elementary school. Most of what she earned paid for groceries and household sundries, while Barry's salary paid for "big ticket items," the mortgage, bills, and savings.

They lived a modest lifestyle, sacrificing luxury items in order to save for retirement. They put most of their money into a small vacation home in Florida, where they planned to move after retirement and live off their savings. Three years shy of retirement, the financial meltdown of 2008 hit, decimating Barry's portfolio. The housing crash devalued their home by 30%, but thankfully, they had paid off their thirty-year mortgage. Unfortunately, their Florida home was only ten years in to a twenty-year mortgage, and the current market value was only 50% of their purchase price, leaving them under water. Barry's manufacturing plant shut down when the company decided to go overseas. At age sixty-two, Barry found himself out of work and without any employment prospects. For the first time, and through no fault of their own, they were in an economic crisis. Thankfully, Tina had her job at the florist, although her arthritis made working with the arrangements increasingly more difficult. Nevertheless, between the mortgage in Florida and the cost of private health insurance, Barry and Tina were struggling to get through the crisis. Their retirement was not only postponed, but nowhere in sight.

Barry and Tina, like thousands of others hit by the recession, were struggling with a completely new reality. The shared shock and loss presented them with an opportunity to grow stronger or break down, but staying the same simply wasn't an option.

***What do you do when everything you dreamed of,
planned and paid for, comes crashing down?***

They experienced the stages of grief during the process. At first, they were in denial about how bad things were getting. They saw home prices in Florida start to sag, but it never occurred to them they would want or need to sell. They were caught completely off guard by the Wall Street crash and bargained on a reasonably quick rebound. By the time the numbers indicated otherwise, it was too late. That's when they got angry. As the truth about individual and corporate greed oozed out in the following weeks and months, their outrage grew. When Barry was let go, he sunk into a depression, the likes of which neither he nor Tina had ever seen.

It was at that point they turned to professionals for help. He went to his doctor for antidepressants, and the two came in for counseling. They needed a place to safely vent their anger and discuss options for moving forward. They hoped to gain some perspective about their life's journey and the unexpected turns it had taken. Ultimately, therapy wasn't going to restore their old economic picture, but it could help them adjust to the new one.

Tina and Barry had a lot going for them as a couple. They respected one another and valued their partnership. They communicated effectively, and they had co-created their shared vision. Because neither had regrets about their choices or the roles each had played, they could build on their strengths to create a new vision. Although their payoff didn't come in the form of an early or easy retirement, they were proud their children were happy, well-educated, employed, and starting families of their own. They felt blessed for what they had accomplished and could now work together to plan their next stage.

Research has demonstrated that hardiness, optimism, and humor are three characteristics that help people rebound in the aftermath of a profoundly stressful life event. Tina and Barry certainly demonstrated all three.

This myth has been in play long before the current economic crisis, and unfortunately, not everyone operating under it is so successful. Meet Dale and Dora, a working class couple with a very proud economic picture. They had no credit card debt, a tight budget, and a small nest egg. It would have been perfect were it not for the knock down, drag out fights they had about money and spending. It was a constant battle for control of the purse strings.

Dale and Dora: Scrounging for Security
Dale was the first person in his very poor family to attend trade school. Five years later, he was a hard worker in the plumbers' union. Dora moved to town for a secretarial position in the County Clerk's office. Her new officemates took her to the local watering hole during her first week in town, where she met Dale. The two discovered they had a lot in common. Both were the first of their families to receive post-secondary education. They enjoyed the same movies and television shows. Dora loved how smart Dale was about money. He was a careful spender, he saved, and he shopped for bargains. She'd never met a man like that. Dale liked that Dora was so easy to please, later reporting a lot of girls demanded flowers and gifts, but not Dora. She'd rather have the money in the bank. Such a low maintenance woman he had never met. The two never looked back. They had a simple wedding because they agreed it would be better to save money for a house. Five years later, they moved into their home and started a family.

Fast-forward sixteen years. They lived without a credit card, and they had a modest nest egg for retirement and a smaller fund for college. What they did not have was either agreement about money matters or peace in their home. They fought about money ALL THE TIME. He wanted to stay on track and see the same amount of money going into savings every month. He controlled the purse strings and gave cash to Dora to spend on the house and children. She did not have access to bank accounts, and Dale required her to save receipts and account for every penny she spent. Though one might expect the food budget to grow as children became teenagers, Dale refused, believing that Dora should be clever enough to make do. Their thirteen-year-old daughter needed clothes and shoes, but again, the budgeted amount set during young childhood "should" have sufficed.

Dale knew he was asking everyone to sacrifice, but no more than he did. He showed off his new winter boots and asked if I liked them. "They look fine," I replied. He then boasted he had found them in a dumpster. "Do you BELIEVE that?" he mused. Dora dropped her head into her hands, ashamed as he revealed the family secret. Dale was a dumpster-diver, which embarrassed the kids, horrified Dora, but "proved" that their family could live on the current budget structure Dale had set.

After getting to know this couple in therapy, it was clear Dale lived in constant fear that he was going to lose his job or sustain an injury that would prevent him from working, leaving his family destitute. His fears meant that he could never have enough money in the bank. He was like a squirrel stashing away for a long, harsh winter that might never come.

Dale's fears drove him to live as though financial devastation had already hit.

Though they had entered the marriage concurring that today's sacrifice was worth tomorrow's security, they hadn't been clear on the *level* of sacrifice. Dale had gone to such an extreme that Dora could no longer buy in to their agreement. She felt Dale was expecting too much of the children. *"They're good kids,"* she reported. *"They help around the house a lot, and they deserve to have some new things."* She knew they had a pretty low social standing because they wore old clothes and couldn't do activities and social events like the other kids. Especially for the sake of their 13-year-old daughter, who was really starting to experience the social effects of her dad's penny-pinching, Dora needed to gain some control over the family's money.

Dale's explanation for his behavior was perfectly reasonable. He did not see himself as controlling. He gave Dora cash every month, which she could spend however she wanted. He posed the question to me, wide-eyed and eager for validation, *"Isn't it BETTER to live without debt?"* I must admit, all else being equal, living without debt seems better than living with debt. However, I'm in the people business, and I work in the world of feelings, behaviors, and consequences. Because actions have consequences, the question must be addressed:

> **Do the *feelings alleviated* by the behavior
> outweigh the *consequences* of the behavior?**

Behaviors, such as tightly controlling the money and scrounging in dumpsters for usable discards, alleviated his anxiety and fears about money. The consequences of those behaviors included the alienation of his family, fights about money, and his children's lowered social standing with their peers. Yes, putting money in the bank reduced his fear that his family wouldn't have enough one day, but it caused profound stress on his relationships with his children and his wife. It wasn't balancing out.

Dale was reluctant to address the root cause of his fears. Growing up in a family that never had enough and getting the message that *a man who can't support his family is not a man,* left Dale in a constant state of anxiety that he would be judged harshly if he could not provide for his family. He also resisted addressing the slew of contradictions, too proud to "owe money to anybody" (i.e., refused to get a credit card), but not too proud to rummage through dumpsters to find clothing, food, and other household items. This was very painful for Dale to think about, because the psychological constructs at work to sustain the behaviors were very deep. Yet, Dora was going to walk out on the marriage or have a nervous breakdown if he didn't change. We addressed his anxiety directly with a combination of visual imagery and relaxation techniques[10] and traditional systematic desensitization.[11] This was a particularly good approach to use with Dale, because he could do a significant amount of practice at home, when he wasn't on the clock with me. I also set them up to meet with a certi-

---

[10]The meditation exercise at the end of Chapter 2 is an example of these techniques. The point is to involve the whole body in getting the autonomic nervous system to stand down, enabling the person to relax the body and mind.

[11]*Systematic Desensitization* remains one of the most effective tools to address fears. It entails generating an "Anxiety Hierarchy" that lists the sources of fear from least to most intense, teaching the person deep relaxation skills, and then helping them move through the list while remaining deeply relaxed.

fied financial planner at a discounted rate, so they could address their family's financial plan with a qualified third party.

With the kids a bit older, Dora was able to work part-time during the day, but working outside of the home meant less time for household chores, which Dale found unacceptable. *"She should be able to make it work,"* he insisted. He didn't want to think about the house, it just needed to be clean and cared for, and that was Dora's responsibility. He would say, *"My mom always made it work, so why can't she?"*

In order to establish a partnership that was going to work for both of them, Dale needed to start sharing responsibilities with Dora, rather than dictating to her the ways in which she needed to tow the line. After much work on his own anxiety, and with the help of some heavy duty communication tools, Dale was able to develop empathy for Dora and become a better roommate, helping around the house as needed. Although harder to do, he eventually trusted her with access to the family bank accounts. He continued to trigger easily over financial challenges that cropped up from time to time, but they were able to communicate and negotiate their way through those challenges.

Dora and Dale remind us that the shared vision is vital, but couples must also share the means to get there, as well.

Our fears should motivate us to do our best, but when they drive us to behavior that hurts our loved ones, it is time to confront them.

After all, *We'll Be Happy When We Get There* assumes you are actually going to complete the journey together, and if it becomes an unsustainable arrangement, you are not going to make it, not together anyway. Dale seemed to believe *"We'll **only** be happy **if** we get there,"* and he lost sight of the importance of happiness along the way. Old messages and anxiety he brought with him from his youth into his adulthood almost cost him his family.

To successfully navigate the journey, couples should regularly evaluate how things are going and plan for what is ahead. I recommend adult members of the family initiate an "Annual Summit" to accomplish this task. It is a helpful framework through which couples can connect, communicate, and plan for the future.

HOW TO HAVE A SUCCESSFUL ANNUAL SUMMIT

Step One: *Schedule your summit.*

Some couples like to work around the calendar year, so they retreat during the winter holidays for their annual summit. Couples raising children often find the summer months, between academic years, a more natural time to plan in anticipation of changes that will come with the new school year. Although the idea of holding the summit while away on a holiday may sound relaxing and lovely, it typically doesn't work out, as vacation days fly by, you are distracted by children and leisure activities, and you will likely find you don't have all the data you need with you. I recommend you leave your laptops and cell phones at home, and enjoy your vacation unencumbered. Relax and recharge as a couple, and then take care of business after you return. If you have children, find a time when they will be out of the house so you can talk freely about family matters. Don't expect "after the children are in bed" to suffice. Everyone is tired in the evening, and I can't imagine a less desirable condition under which to begin the process. You would be wise to schedule a series of two or three meetings spread over the course of a week or two, because you may need a breather during the process, a time when you can step away to reflect on something that has come up, gather additional data, or just sleep on an idea.

Step Two: *Plan your agenda and gather your data.*

Think about what issues you *need* to discuss, like children, careers, and money, and what issues you *want* to discuss, like leisure activities, and communication. Each person should contribute agenda items, which, in and of itself, is more than some couples do to remain actively engaged in the process of their own relationship. If you come up with an item that requires some legwork, take responsibility for getting that done in advance. For example, if you need to have some trees removed from your yard and you think this is the year to do it, consult with professionals about cost, timing, and any city ordinances you might need to know. The expense can be worked into the budget, and the process can be anticipated and scheduled accordingly. Some couples like to build the agenda together. Either way, the summit will be most productive if both people know what is on the agenda in advance and each takes responsibility to gather necessary data.

The whole point of this meeting is to frame out, as best as you can, a plan for the upcoming year, and you will naturally base your plan on the past year's experience. Bring the family calendar from the previous year as a reference, along with any other schedule-related paperwork. For example, if your daughter's band is going on a trip in the coming year, have the materials with you, as they will provide important dates, fundraising details, and deadlines.

When in doubt, include anything related to dates or dollars.

Summarize bank accounts and balances so you can easily see where your money is and how it flows on a weekly or monthly basis. If you have an electronic accounting system, print out income and expense reports so it is clear how it all balanced out in the previous year. If you don't have your family spending captured in a software program, go through bank statements and canceled checks to find out where your money went.

Step Three: *Hold your meeting and get to work.*

The past year in review: Was it good for you? Start with a basic question:

How did _____ work out last year?

Fill in the blank with anything from *Susie's extracurricular activities* to *Mom's employment at the bookstore*. "How it worked out" takes into consideration a basic cost/benefit discussion that includes the financial, personal, and emotional costs and benefits (e.g., *it was expensive but she really got a lot out of it, learned valuable life lessons, and made some good friends*). The point is to determine if it is an activity you are going to work in again, and that depends on the answer to this question:

Was it worth the time and expense?

The stage is set for people to get defensive, as this review is an opportunity to take a bird's-eye view of the whole picture and assess what could have been done differently. Arguments that involve the "shouldn't haves" will certainly sabotage the process.

"Maybe you shouldn't have spent $500 on fishing tackle this year."
"Well, maybe you shouldn't have blown so much cash at the salon!"
*"Did you have to play 18-holes of golf **every** Friday?"*
*"Did Anna need a new dress for **every** Bat Mitzvah she attended?"*

There's no need for this kind of back-and-forth because the bottom line will be revealed when you review the budget, and if the numbers didn't add up, you'll *both* have to look at your spending and decide what sacrifices you'll be willing to make in the coming year. *"Maybe I **shouldn't** have spent money on _____."* If you find yourself getting angry or defensive during this process, step away for a few minutes, go somewhere comfortable, and breathe. Count your blessings.

You've both committed to this process for the sake of the family, and sometimes the truth hurts.

Take a relationship inventory. The Annual Summit is a good opportunity to take a relationship inventory. *How did **we** do this year? Did we spend enough time together? In what ways did you support me? In what ways could I have been more supportive of you? Was there anything you wanted to do but didn't feel you could?* Those in healthy relationships will be more than willing and able to have this conversation; they will be eager to learn how to improve.

If you or your partner let *ego* get in the way, you may need some professional help. Here's how to check for that. Let's say your wife expresses concern about your communication. If you react by defending how busy you are at work, then your ego has just hijacked the conversation, making it about *you* and your schedule rather than your spouse and her need to feel connected with you. If this pattern sounds familiar, it might be worth visiting a therapist to work on non-defensive communication. We will revisit this in Chapter 9.

As you come out of the review, you will have a general sense of what worked and what did not work for you and your family. If everyone was overscheduled and stressed, you need to find ways to scale back on activities in the coming year. If you and your spouse disconnected, you need to make the relationship a higher priority. If the budget did not balance out, you will have to find ways to trim spending or increase earning. Don't panic. It's all good knowledge to have, and it will serve to inform decisions as you plan ahead. Keep in mind; you are only planning for the next year. If a compromise doesn't work out as you hope it will, you will rework it at next year's meeting.

Some of you will be astounded at this point, because you simply hadn't realized how *out of balance* you were living. This mindfulness alone puts you in a better position than you were in before. It may *feel* worse, because ignorance was bliss. In the long run, you are better off discovering and recalibrating. Your goal is to be better positioned by next year's summit. So even if you are not where you want to be, you can feel good about getting on the right track.

Plan ahead. Now it's time to address the upcoming calendar, and you can start by mapping out anticipated activities, events, holidays, and travel. Are you or the kids adding or dropping activities? There are many excellent extracurricular activities for children to experience, but they need to be in balance. Maybe Jimmy can't play basketball this fall, if he's already committed to soccer and piano lessons. Extracurricular involvement must be considered in the context of the child's individual academic needs. Not all kids can juggle after-school activities with homework and reading requirements. This is an opportunity to assess how the children should be spending their time, and how the parents will work to support their academic needs as well as coordinate driving and attending extracurricular events.

This is also the time to consider what the two of you can do together. Look at your park district's catalogue to see if there are classes or sports you'd both enjoy. How can you and your spouse support each other's leisure activities? I know a family of six in which both parents like to be involved with two of their children in the local community theater. As it is not practical for both to be in a show at the same time, they take turns, so that one is participating with the children in the show, while one is home parenting the children not involved in the show. The next show, they switch, which is exactly the point of communicating and making agreements from year to year.

Create a budget. It is hard to plan for leisure and extracurricular activities without getting into the budget. Some hobbies, like cooking, might readily fit into the household budget, whereas more expensive hobbies, like boating or golf, may take more planning. Identify what you'd like to do and have the anticipated costs on hand as you work out a budget for the year. For example, golf is expensive, but seasonal in some parts of the country. If you save for it during the cold months, it won't be such a burden during the summer. Setting up financial goals and finding pathways to achieve them requires patience and persistence. Look at the numbers from the previous year and address the anticipated changes. Understand who is spending what and how you are saving for long-term needs (e.g., college savings and retirement) as well as short-term crises (e.g., a blown water heater or auto repair). This may require hiring a professional financial planner. It doesn't matter how big or modest your financial picture; you will likely need help to work the numbers out, and a financial planner is a wonderful investment if you've not done this before.

The Annual Summit is not a perfect process, and there will likely be moments of tension and discouragement. Be good listeners for each other and support one another during the process. Every detail may not get worked out, but the framework will get you started on the right foot, mindful of each other, your family, time, and money.

CONCLUSION

Together, the *Barter Economy* and the *We'll Be Happy When We Get There* myths account for a lot of the wheeling and dealing people do in relationships in order to get their needs met. The Annual Summit is an excellent tool to address all of these deals, getting them out on the table for scrutiny and discussion. If defensiveness or secrecy sabotages the process, get help right away. A professional therapist can help you work through whatever is blocking you from participating with open minds and open hearts. These myths also show us how we *can* be happy living under them, as long as they don't go bust. If they do, our ability to navigate a new path forward may very well depend on the strength of our communication and partnership prior to confronting the unexpected obstacle.

MYTH 6: CHILDREN WILL BRING US CLOSER TOGETHER

Boys will be boys and men are men, but once a man becomes a father, he becomes a *dad*. He leaves immaturity and personal needs behind to embark on the great adventure of *parenthood*. Popular movies have perpetuated this idea for decades. In the 1980s, it was Kevin Bacon in *She's Having a Baby*. In the 1990s, it was Hugh Grant in *Nine Months*. Most recently, Seth Rogen in *Knocked Up* was the hapless guy magically transformed during a 90-minute journey. The common theme? Babies awaken a man's inner grown-up. And of course, who is there to finally enjoy the new man this guy has become, but his *wife*. *"And they lived happily ever after ..."*

At the heart of this myth is the (mostly) subconscious belief that you and your partner do not have exactly what it takes for a great relationship, but if you had more in common, or a project to do together, you would. This may be true, and if you're talking about taking up tennis, joining a book club, or any "together" activity that involves high fun and low stakes, I recommend it. As far as bringing a child into this world to raise together, however, nothing could be further from the truth. Children are a blessing, and happy couples can find levels of intimacy they didn't know existed through the journey of parenting. Yet, this does not negate the fact that babies are hard work, and they will magnify any weaknesses in the relationship.

Among the many different circumstances that bring this myth into play, we will focus on two. In the first, we find women ready to settle down but partnered with men who aren't. Maybe he has a wandering eye or *he's just not that into you.* Maybe he's committed to getting a good start on his career or he needs to finish his education. Whatever the distraction may be, he's not taking time to nurture the relationship, and she's in a panic that she won't be able to hold on to him.

In the second, we find married couples who do share a commitment and love for each other but still feel disconnected and discontent. They share a false belief that having a child is the answer to the marital problem.

Estelle and Chad: Children Will Keep Him Home

Meet Estelle. She was a beautiful young woman, although she struggled to see that. Despite the problems she had with self-esteem, she was educated, gainfully employed, and living on her own in the city. She thought Chad, her boyfriend and a successful trader, was a bit out of her league. She loved his self-confidence, and after years of dating, he still flirted with her, brought her flowers, and reassured her that SHE was the only one for him. In many ways, he was the Prince Charming she had waited for: handsome, rich, and romantic. How could she expect such a man NOT to eye the occasional waitress or flirt with coworkers once in a while? That's just part of the package. She believed him to be a man with integrity who would never cross the line. Their engagement saw a bit of drama; in fact, they both identify it as the time the arguing began. She expected him to care about the wedding and he expected his romantic gestures would buy him the option of only being involved when it suited his schedule. Tension really flared when Estelle and her mother happened upon Chad shamelessly (and obviously) flirting with a staff member at their club. Her mother leaned toward Estelle and sang in a whisper, "You're going to have to keep an eye on this one!" reinforcing several unfortunate ideas in Estelle's mind:

> *(1) A certain amount of inappropriate behavior is to be expected from men.*
> *(2) Estelle didn't deserve any better.*
> *(3) It was somehow going to be Estelle's responsibility to keep Chad reined in!*

Years later, as Estelle cried in my office because her marriage was over, she identified that as the moment she pushed down her inner voice that told her to run. Her ego told her she could manage Chad. He was so close to being everything she wanted that if she could just reel him in a bit tighter, he would get on board and all would be well. Having children with him was a deliberate part of that plan. Maybe he wouldn't settle down for her, but he certainly would once children were involved. He wasn't keen on starting a family right away, but Estelle wasn't 100% reliable about taking her birth control pills, and within a year of the wedding, their first child was born. Estelle was quite happy to leave her job and stay home with the baby, and a few years later, she had their second. To her dismay, she and the children spent a lot of time alone. Still wanting to keep him engaged, she worked hard to make their house a haven for Chad. She fed and bathed the children before he was expected home each evening. They played quietly or read together for hours, waiting for his arrival. She believed that if she and the children were perfect for him and easy to be with, he would want to spend more time together, but on most nights, the children were asleep before he arrived home.

As the kids grew, Chad was fairly involved with them on weekends, coaching their teams, but less so during the week, only attending school functions when he could get away from the office. There was virtually no co-parenting time, and Estelle was certain he had no idea what the daily grind of parenting was really like. Further, he didn't seem interested in learning.

Through the years, Chad and Estelle hadn't changed very much as a couple. She continued to desire a closeness with him that seemed just out of reach, and she settled for the same "dating" behaviors, complete with romantic gestures and trips, as a substitute.

His gestures were comforting signs of commitment, so she never questioned his loyalty. It never occurred to her that Chad would be unfaithful. She worked hard to prevent him from having any reason to step out. She made herself and the children everything a man could want: lots of rewards and very low maintenance. Still, he often went to Vegas with friends, worked late, and went out after work. She couldn't manage him. Yet, he continued to be romantic and extend the grand gestures, which reassured her that her inner voice was wrong. Her marriage was just fine.

It was the Monday after a romantic weekend away. As she unpacked for them, she discovered he left his cell phone behind that morning when it vibrated on the bed under a pile of clothes. She had a moment of panic. Chad relied heavily on his cell phone for business. Even after work and on weekends, he was attached to it. She worried he could not function at work without it and was mentally rearranging her day so she could drive it down to his office. She didn't mean to read the incoming text, but the phone was in her hand and she glanced down. She had to read it several times to make sense of what she was seeing. The incoming text read,
"Hey Babe, missed u. Work L8 and c."

As the shock wore off, Estelle wondered where she went wrong. There were several indications along the way, some of which were all around her, but the most important one came from inside. For years, her inner voice had warned her he was not *the one*.

Sometimes that inner voice speaks in such a whisper it's hard to hear, while our response, **"I can manage this,"** booms from within. Neither your marriage nor your spouse should be something you need to manage. Nurture, love, and attend to? Yes. But manage? No. Get help or get out.

Estelle and Chad arrived for couple's therapy, but I suspected it was not going to last long. There was something incredibly condescending in the way he spoke to her, and the betrayal had shaken Estelle out of complacency. He wanted to get back to the way things had been, but that option was no longer on the table, as Estelle had experienced an awakening that would never allow her to go back. After about three months of half-heartedly trying to work things out, Estelle decided she had enough and filed for divorce. She joined a divorce support group and found tremendous comfort getting to know the other women in the group — smart, funny, capable women who really hadn't deserved the raw deal handed them by their ex-husbands. Through the course of individual therapy, she realized she didn't need to worry about being able to trust another man, as had been her concern at the outset. Our work together empowered her to trust herself, and she knew she could count on her own inner voice.

Estelle had no regrets for the time she spent in her marriage. Without the marriage, she wouldn't have been given the gift of her children, and although single parenthood was extraordinarily challenging, it was also her greatest source of joy. For Estelle, her belief that children would strengthen the marriage was clearly one-sided. Our next case involves a couple who shared that belief.

Garrett and Gina's Perfect Plan

Garrett and Gina came in to improve their communication and figure out why they argued so much. They had been married and trying to conceive for three years. The stress and anxiety of their fertility issues weighed very heavily on both of them. No one else in either of their families had any trouble having babies. People were starting to ask questions. Because it was a source of pain and embarrassment for them, they weren't open to their support networks. In fact, they traveled across three towns to seek therapy so no one would find out. By the time we were in session together, they were bursting to tell their stories. No matter how I encouraged them to breathe, relax, and trust that there would be time enough for me to learn the important information, they were anxious and convinced I needed to hear their story right away so I could understand their pain.

Let me pause the case here for a moment to remind you of the intake process I addressed at the end of Chapter 2. Garrett and Gina's presentation during this intake is a good example of a couple eager to get their story out. *Getting the story out* can feel good, but a skilled therapist won't need a lot of information from you to empathize with your pain; they will feel it. They are tuned in on an emotional level, and how you are *feeling* won't require much explanation. In order to understand where the pain is coming from, a therapist will thoughtfully ask appropriate questions. However, before getting to *the story*, the therapist needs to get you grounded in the session first. This is an important step towards helping you cope with the issue. As the sessions unfold, the therapist will ask more probing questions. Please know:

The therapist is not asking you to justify your feelings. She (or he) needs to understand where the feelings come from in order to help you process them.

Garrett and Gina wanted to tell me their story, which is understandable. Unexpected fertility issues can be emotionally devastating to newlyweds, and in their case, they were also dealing with three years of built up frustration with their bodies and each other.

Garrett and Gina met after college, when they both worked in the city. It was a very exciting time in their lives, and they were perfectly matched. Both from large, Italian-Catholic families, it was almost too good to be true. They each had wanted to live in the city for a few years after college, get careers going, find a spouse, and then move to the suburbs to raise their own big family. They used every minute of their eighteen-month engagement to plan an elaborate wedding, with all the traditions both families expected. She moved into his condo after the wedding, and when his lease expired a year later, they moved to a four-bedroom home in the suburbs. It needed some fixing up, but it would eventually be perfect for their anticipated brood. She composed her letter of resignation, and planned to submit it as soon as she got pregnant. Until then, she and Garrett commuted by train into the city to work by day, and retreated to their suburban do-it-yourself projects and baby making by night.

The arguments were few and far between at first. What color should the walls be in the dining room? How could you possibly think Bond *movies are better than* Bourne *movies? It was light and playful. As the months turned into years, arguments became more pointed. Why do we have to spend so much time with your parents? Why don't we talk on the train anymore? By the time they were in my office in a heated discussion trying to identify their issues, their hostility could not be contained. He blurted out, "She's only interested in me when she's ovulating," to which she retorted that he was lucky she wanted him at all, given how he'd let himself go.*

Garrett and Gina had a plan. It was a perfect plan, and they had found the perfect match in each other to carry it out; there just wasn't much deeply connecting them *beyond* that plan. Adversity reveals character, and they hadn't had much adversity up to this point. She didn't know he got mean when he was angry, and he didn't know she would never retreat from an argument. They hadn't cared that their taste in movies and cuisine was wildly different, because while dating, they spent most of their leisure time with friends, taking advantage of all that the city had to offer twenty-somethings. They hadn't really gotten to know each other. They had lived from one distraction to the next — the thrill of the relationship, the wedding, moving to the suburbs, and nesting.

It was time for the next distraction, the first baby, and when that didn't happen, the couple had nothing of substance between them to support the relationship.

We worked together for a few months, helping them build their relationship and develop better communication. I also helped them utilize their support network by carefully selecting confidants from among their closest family and friends.

They finally felt comfortable seeking the assistance of a fertility specialist. After a series of tests, the results were a shock. Garrett and Gina had an unforeseen chemistry issue. Although each could conceive a child, it was virtually impossible for them to conceive together without medical intervention. They were devastated by this news. Gina, now twenty-eight, was upset they hadn't found out sooner. In her mind, she wasted over three precious, fertile years. She blamed Garrett for that, because he had resisted medical intervention, believing it was all going to unfold according to God's plan. Although they were both practicing Catholics, Garrett was more conservative than Gina, and he struggled with the notion that they would have to create a family in medical facilities. He just didn't feel right about that, and Gina had no patience for Garrett's struggle. Ultimately, they just didn't have a lot of fight left in them. They were divorced within the year, and their marriage was annulled by the Church.

Garrett and Gina had counted on children to seal the deal of their life together. That is a lot of pressure to put on a baby — born or unborn!

Both of these cases share the misconception that a relationship can *hinge* on children and be okay. Having children doesn't change the relationship, except to increase the pressure to have a good one. Discussions about children must be open and honest, and you have to take your partner's words at face value. Most importantly, you have to love your spouse and your relationship with or without children.

WHEN CHILDREN *DON'T* BRING US CLOSER TOGETHER

Because *"Children Will Bring Us Closer Together"* often leads to children in an unhappy marriage, an unfortunate (but not unexpected) outcome is a marriage in which parents believe, *"We must stay together for the sake of the children."* I have heard many reasonable explanations as to why. Some parents are afraid the split would emotionally devastate their children.[12] A family circumstance might drive this belief. For example, couples who have children with profound mental, emotional, or physical issues may seek a way to stay together out of necessity, because it really does take the coordination of two high functioning parents to meet the special needs of their children. In other cases, one spouse worries about the emotional stability of the other, and consequently stays in the marriage because he fears his spouse couldn't handle parenting alone. On the other hand, some parents believe they cannot be good parents until they are happy people, and they choose divorce as a step towards happiness and *better* parenting. Others assert that they do not want their children to grow up thinking *this* is what marriage is supposed to look like and divorce to teach children about integrity and decision making.

I've heard lots of arguments for and against staying married for the sake of the children. I don't believe there is a clear-cut, right or wrong answer, and it is never the role of the therapist to tell a couple what to do. Here are some of the questions I pose to clients as they determine if staying in the marriage is really the right move for the sake of the children:

1. Can you live peacefully together until the children are grown? This is almost a trick question because, even when the answer is an emphatic *yes,* it rarely works out this way. It does not matter if both

---

[12]Unfortunately, the same parents who are worried about emotionally devastating their children are often unconcerned about the impact of the children witnessing the emotionally (and sometimes physically) abusive fights that transpire between mom and dad.

are committed to having a peaceful home. If the decision to divorce is one-sided, the pain of the abandoned spouse will almost always prompt discord.

2. Do you trust one another with money and spending? Although the laws vary from state to state, it might be the case that you and your spouse are equally responsible for the marital assets and debt. If one person maxes out the credit cards while married, both are on the hook for the bill. If you don't trust your spouse with money, it might be better to have the courts intervene, so the money flows where it's supposed to as a means to protect the children's needs, present and future.

3. Are you going to continue an intimate relationship or live a celibate life? If two people don't want to be married anymore, quite often they aren't interested in each other sexually, but why consider celibacy? Ideally, you aspire to be role models for your children, and if you are together in marriage, you need to live with integrity in that decision. Some couples fantasize a sort of "Sonny and Cher" arrangement, living separate lives under the same roof.[13] That rarely works out. The children tend to discover this open arrangement, leaving them to grieve their parents' break up while knowing their parents were lying to them. Further, they have "learned" marriage doesn't have to be taken too seriously. Ultimately, the arrangement doesn't spare the children's feelings and, arguably, makes the situation worse.

4. Will you cooperatively co-parent? Will you continue to have family time (such as meals and family vacations) that includes everyone? Will you take turns engaging with the children, in which case, will you be accountable to each other when it's not your turn on the *parenting clock?* Children usually catch on when their parents start pulling the Clark Kent/Superman routine, never being in the same place at the same time. The children notice, and the parents are posi-

---

[13]You may or may not recall in the 1970s, when Sonny and Cher had a hit television series, they kept up the facade of a happily married couple to protect their public image. They divided the house in two, and each coupled with other partners while living under the same roof.

tioned to create more and more elaborate excuses as to why they can't both be in attendance at any given time.

5. Are you really doing this to protect the children? Children are surprisingly resilient, and many schools and community organizations offer support groups and counseling for kids going through major life transitions. Parents are motivated to protect their children from divorce, but in my experience, children traumatized during the divorce process are reacting to their parents' bad behavior, not to the divorce, per se.

The divorce process tends to bring out the worst in people, and some can't seem to help themselves. Their emotional pain bubbles over into very destructive behavior, and they use the children to hurt each other. Contrary to protecting their children, these parents hurt them by disclosing details, confiding feelings, and manipulating their children's emotions in an effort to get them to take sides. These are the destructive behaviors that will cause long-term harm to your children and your relationship with them. *You have to love your children more than you hate your ex.* You have to find it in you to put them first and really protect them. Children need both parents to love them enough to leave them out of it.

The best you can do to protect your children is to prepare yourself for the major transition about to take place. The *family* will need help along the way, no doubt, because the children will have very important feelings to process as they experience their own transition grief. It may be difficult for parents to be there for their children, when they, themselves, have so much of their own pain to process.

Lindsay's Transition Twister

Elisabeth Kübler-Ross[14] identified five stages of grief experienced during the process of death and dying. I use these stages in my practice to help normalize the myriad of emotions experienced by people in transition. Let's examine the transition of ten-year-old Lind-

---

[14]Elisabeth Kübler-Ross, M.D., introduced these stages in her classic book *On Death and Dying,* published in 1969.

say during her parent's separation and divorce to understand the constructs at work.

Denial is the brain's failure to accept what it sees and hears as real. "It just isn't true."

Rachel and Richard were separated and getting a divorce. Richard had moved into a guest bedroom six months earlier. They had stopped going on family outings, and each parent took Lindsay on separate vacations during that time. Lindsay was a precocious ten-year-old and wise beyond her years. Still, she accepted her parents' explanation that Dad found the guest bed more comfortable than his own. She didn't question the business meetings and other excuses that kept one parent away from her at a time. Lindsay was in denial that there was anything wrong with her parents' marriage. When they sat her down in the living room to break the news, Lindsay shook her head. "It just can't be true."

Bargaining occurs when the person tries to strike deals to change the outcome. "If I am well behaved, you will change your minds."

Over the next several weeks, as the news started to sink in for Lindsay, she became a model citizen in her home. She kept her own room clean and volunteered to do extra chores around the house. She prepared snacks and set them out on the table, inviting her parents to come and join her. She got all A's on her report card, and brought her parents into the kitchen together to share this news. Lindsay's behavior reflected her bargaining. "If I'm perfect, you won't have to get divorced."

When bargaining doesn't resolve the issue, the next stage is **anger**. "Fine, get divorced. See if I care!"

Richard moved into an apartment a few streets away from their house. Lindsay refused to visit him there; in fact, she stopped speaking to him altogether. She was angry. Rachel got a call from Lindsay's teacher, who reported Lindsay was being mean to other chil-

dren at recess. Rachel sat down with Lindsay after school to talk with her about her feelings, but Lindsay would have none of it.

"There's nothing to talk about. I'm fine."

"Your teacher doesn't think so, you stomp around here in a terrible mood, and you won't talk to Daddy. That doesn't sound fine to me."

"You guys are the ones getting a divorce. Why should I care?"

When anger, like denial and bargaining, fails to affect the situation, it often leads to **depression**. "There's nothing I can do about it. It's hopeless."

Lindsay had experienced denial, bargaining, and anger, and she was getting emotionally drained as the weeks went by. As her emotional resources depleted and the reality of the divorce set in, she started to get sad. Her appetite decreased, she lost interest in her friends, and she was tired during the day. One night, Rachel overheard Lindsay crying in her room. She tapped on the door and poked her head into the room.

"May I come in?"

Lindsay didn't have any fight left in her. She nodded, and allowed Rachel to sit on the bed and hold her as she cried. "I can't believe this is happening to us. I miss Daddy being here and I miss our family," she stammered through her sobs.

Eventually, the sadness yields to **acceptance**. "I guess this is the way it is."

Lindsay attended the divorce support group in school every week and eventually started to feel like herself again. She was surprised at how homey her Dad's apartment was, and she didn't mind spending time there. She was glad to see her parents attend her sports events, and although she felt a pang of sadness when they left in different cars, she knew they were all okay. "Thanks for coming, Daddy. See you on Saturday."

Lindsay's story unfolded in a linear way, and she transitioned through denial, bargaining, anger, depression, and acceptance in that order. In reality, the transitions can be very messy. Also remember that everyone in the family has their own transition going on. Rachel and Richard started theirs long before telling their child. In fact, parents often want the divorce to remain secret as part of their denial. They cannot face the pain of their community finding out they've failed in their marriage. The process takes time. If you have experienced divorce, perhaps you can relate. You may recall days when you woke up feeling good, only to burst into tears at the slightest provocation. You may have felt like extending an olive branch, only to fly into a rage when a legal document arrived in the mail. Feelings come and go quickly, and you can experience multiple feelings at the same time. This is all *normal*. I think of these feelings like dots on a Twister®[15] mat. We have columns of Yellow (denial), Green (bargaining), Red (anger), and Blue (depression) dots, as is on the traditional mat, and we add a purple column, to indicate *acceptance*. Just like the game of Twister®, parts of you can be all over the mat. Hands and feet spread over different colored dots, and you never know when the spinner is going to land on a new color, sending you into motion once again. At the start of the process, you may spend most of your time on the yellow and green dots, with the occasional stray foot landing on red or blue. Then you might find yourself spending more time on blue and red dots. At some point, you realize you landed on a purple dot, and it feels good, but the spinner is still moving, and you might not stay in that good place very long. Eventually, you find yourself on the purple dots more frequently and staying there longer, with the occasional slip back onto yellow or red dots. I call this *Transition Twister*. This change process takes you from an old reality to a new reality; in this case, from *married* to *divorced*.

It takes two people to get married, but only one to get a divorce. This reality can generate very different transition experiences for members of the same family. The spouse seeking the divorce may have had months or years to work through denial and bargaining, perhaps even anger and depression. The spouse being left may jump quickly from denial to anger upon hearing the news. There is high risk

---

[15]Twister is a registered trademark of the Milton Bradley Company, Springfield, MA. Patented July 8, 1969, #3,454,279.

for extreme discord that could potentially harm the children. It is important to seek professional help to process the pain of this transition.

EXERCISE

Identify some of your major life events and disappointments, for example, moving, getting your first job, getting fired for the first time, falling in love, getting dumped. Think about your emotional experience during these big changes. What was your general response style? Did you bargain for a different outcome? Were you depressed? In Chapter 5, I introduced the personal qualities hardiness, resilience, and humor, which can ease transitions. Were these qualities present or absent during these big transitions?

If you are currently struggling with a major life transition, I suggest you purchase a five-section notebook and label each section with one of the five feelings in Transition Twister. Get into the habit of flipping to the section labeled with whatever you are feeling and start writing. Do not judge or criticize. Just get your feelings out. As time goes on, you will be able to read earlier entries and observe your own progress, and you will see the number of entries in the *acceptance* section go up as you move through the change process.

CONCLUSION

In this chapter, we looked at the ways children can be used by parents in an attempt to strengthen a relationship, maintain a marriage, and keep a marriage together past its natural expiration date. None of this is okay. In the developmental milestones you experience throughout the lifespan, having children is among the most profound. If you are doing it right, it is among the most selfless. In order to do right by your children, you must aspire to be a healthy, high-functioning adult, *able* to put the children first. I'm not talking about being perfect, and certainly not pretending to be perfect. You must be earnest in your effort to raise children in a loving and peaceful home. You may need help getting yourself and your relationships where they need to be, especially if your emotional resources have been depleted through the painful process of divorce.

MYTH 7:
LOVE WILL KEEP US TOGETHER

What is *love?* I don't ask rhetorically or sarcastically. Pause and think about *love* as a noun, a thing. Love is a *construct* so deeply connected to emotions, we rarely try to understand it; we just feel it. To overanalyze would wreck it somehow.

But what IS it?

Pause now, and think about romantic partners you've had in your life. Take a few minutes and describe your feelings and behaviors in those relationships. Were you *in love?* How did you know?

LOVE AS ATTACHMENT

Dictionary definitions characterize *love* as attachment and affection. In the 1970s, social psychologist Zick Rubin distinguished liking from loving using three components: intimacy, caring, and attachment. Our ability to *attach* to another person is key; it's also important to the survival of our species. Parental attachment, the first love experienced by little humans as they enter this world, is profound. Parents' hard-wired love for their children outweighs their need for basics, like sleep. It is truly all consuming, and babies love it! After nine long months of waiting, parent and child finally meet face to face, and babies are born ready to attach. They prefer the sight of human faces to other objects. They mirror facial expressions and sounds within days. The attachment instinct is necessary for their very survival, as they suckle for nourishment and comfort. *They must attach to survive.*

The attachment/detachment process we must navigate our whole lives begins during infancy. As babies grow, each step of human development is one of detachment as they become autonomous physically, emotionally, intellectually, and eventually, financially. This series of detachments, although messy and often painful, is also necessary so that they may leave home, reattach with others, and start their own families.

Reattachment can be glorious! Many fondly recall the start of their romantic relationships. They stayed up all night talking, flirting, laughing, staring — gladly letting the world continue without them because nothing was as interesting or cool as this fascinating new person. It's quite reminiscent of a mother and baby's first days together, so thrilling to finally get to know the one they waited so long to meet. It's all spirit and no ego. Other obligations (unpaid bills, our jobs, other relationships, favorite T.V. shows) seem completely unimportant when the ecstasy of new love finds us. We experience the clarity of unconditional love — a strong attachment and a profound affection based on total, mutual acceptance. It isn't long before the rest of the world catches up and we have to attend to more earthly matters, but this intense experience leaves lifelong memories, regardless of the long-term outcome of the relationship.

The human bond we call *attachment* can be a powerful motivator. It keeps us connected to loved ones through difficult times. But it can also keep us stuck in unhealthy relationships. No matter how much we fight, we will stay together because we love each other. No addiction, betrayal, or indignity will turn me away because *I love you, and our love will keep us together.*

Jay and Jessica: Bad Habits in Love

Jay and Jessica met in college when his fraternity hosted a fundraiser with her sorority. They served on the same subcommittee, which required lots of meetings, emails, and phone calls. They felt an instant connection, and their first date was magical. They stayed out all night at the lake, looking up at the stars, talking about everything under the sun, and laughing about the scandal that would erupt if their friends knew where they were.

Jay and Jessica were both very passionate people; they worked hard and played hard. At times, this translated to volatility in their relationship. While in school, their fights were legendary around campus. They screamed at each other, threw things around, and occasionally broke things deliberately. One time, a misunderstood text message from a lab partner landed his cell phone on the roof of the library. Later they laughed about it. He loved that he meant so much to her (and he was impressed with her arm), and she loved that he was man enough to fight for her. During these episodes, they had no concern who was watching, which is how they became well known around campus. Crowds would gather but have no affect on them, whatsoever.

Neither Jay nor Jessica saw anything wrong with their behavior. They were deeply in love and the relationship was worth the fights. Predictably, the fights were worse when either or both of them were over served at parties, which happened often in college. They liked the drama. They liked the attention. And they liked that they had this special relationship that others just didn't understand. Two years later, they were graduated, deeply in love, and married.

DESTRUCTIVE ATTACHMENT

There is no doubt these two were attached, but was it a healthy attachment? They shared great affection, but they also raged at each other. There are different explanations for this discord. Some might argue they subconsciously orchestrated these fights to rekindle the passion and recharge the relationship. It might be argued these were two narcissists who simply needed unconditional devotion from each other and attention from everyone else. When a couple's attachment to each other is unhealthy, you might hear professionals call it *enmeshment* or even *codependence* without a full explanation. Let's unpack those terms.

Enmeshment is a style of attachment in which people wrap their identities and lives together so tightly they both have a hard time getting along on their own. In the opposite, detached relationships, the two are so independent of one another, it's hard to see any connections at all. Healthy relationships live somewhere in between. The connections are there, and they are clear, but each partner can function pretty well independently. *Codependence* involves excessive caretaking, often putting one's needs below the needs of the other person. These behaviors may be okay in small doses, but when one partner routinely sacrifices *self* for *other,* that's codependence. Codependent relationships usually have an enmeshed attachment, which is why the words are often heard together.

Codependence is common when one partner has an addiction. The alcoholic, for example, engages in destructive behavior, and the spouse works overtime to keep the family working, over-functioning in whatever ways are necessary to compensate for the alcoholic's under-functioning. *Love will keep us together* is a lovely idea, but it's also the codependent's battle cry. *I will love you no matter how bad you are for me or how bad we are for each other!*

LOVE IS MORE THAN ATTACHMENT

Robert Sternberg's[16] Triangular Theory of Love is helpful in understanding the complexities of relationships. The points of the triangle are Intimacy, Passion, and Commitment, and the quality of the love relationship depends on the presence and strength of each of the three components. Intimacy without passion or commitment is a close friendship. Passion without intimacy or commitment is an unhealthy state of infatuation. Commitment alone, in the absence of intimacy or passion, is a very lonely love, Sternberg calls *empty*. Different combinations of the components create different qualities of love. Intimacy and passion with no commitment is *romantic love.* Intimacy and commitment without passion is *companionate love,* and passion and commitment without intimacy is *fatuous love,* as is the case when a whirlwind romance leads to a fast commitment, without time for true intimacy to take hold.

Ideally, all three are present in the relationship, and the resulting *consummate* love offers intimacy, passion, and commitment.

This is a helpful framework, but it only tells part of the story. The complexities of human nature make love an exceedingly difficult construct because each of these components can be experienced in unhealthy ways instead of *or in conjunction with* healthy ways. Healthy and unhealthy are not mutually exclusive. Let's try to understand this by looking at them one at a time.

---

[16]Robert Sternberg is best known for his Triarchic Theory of Intelligence.

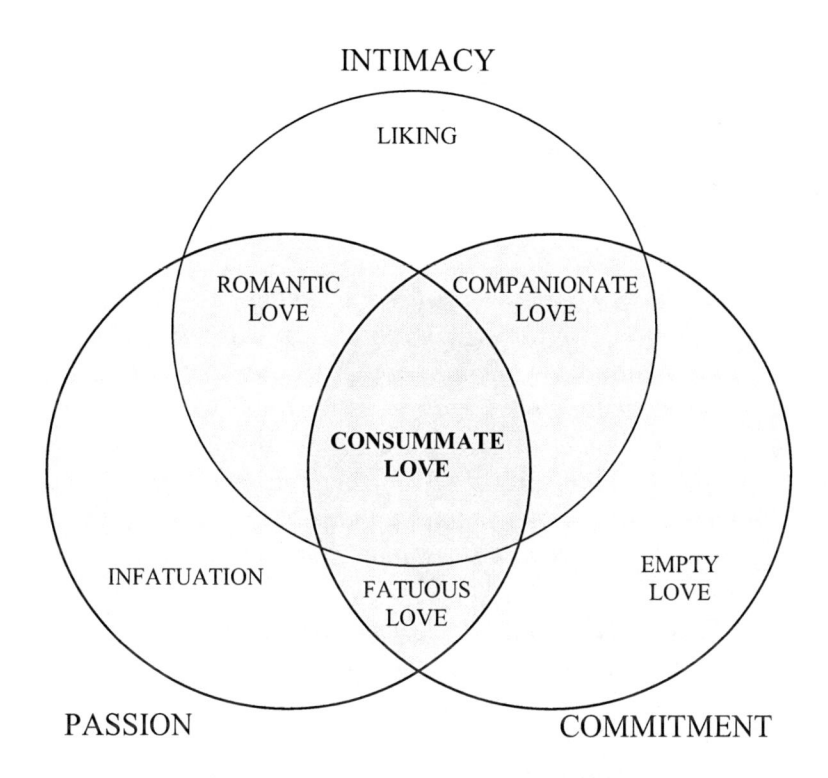

```
                    INTIMACY
                     LIKING

        ROMANTIC          COMPANIONATE
          LOVE                LOVE


                   CONSUMMATE
                      LOVE


    INFATUATION     FATUOUS         EMPTY
                     LOVE            LOVE


    PASSION                      COMMITMENT
```

A Venn diagram of the components of love, based
on the theory by Robert Sternberg.

Passion, as an emotion, is experienced with physiological arousal; in other words, the body gets involved. Heart rate, breathing, sweating, and butterflies in the stomach are all signs of a passionate response, and although you can love passionately, you can also hate passionately. Rage is a very passionate and destructive emotion, and those butterflies can easily be experienced as gut-wrenching knots. The same autonomic nervous system is responsible for both.

Likewise, intimacy can be tricky. Although ideally two people are open and honest and the intimacy is grounded in real life, in reality people aren't open and honest with themselves or with each other all the time. You may experience your partner as a "projected reality" — the person you *want* him to be — more than the person he really is. Alternatively, you may conceal certain aspects of yourself, mainly for fear of rejection, which prevents your partner from experiencing genuine intimacy with you. Even commitment can be unhealthy, if your need to be committed to the person clouds your judgment about safety and common sense.

This myth, *Love Will Keep Us Together*, can block a couple's motivation to change what is harmful or hurtful about the relationship. Let's turn back to Jay and Jessica, twelve years after college, as they are awakening to the realization that something is not right in their relationship.

Jay and Jessica came in for therapy feeling guilty about the home they were creating for their children. There was too much fighting, but they didn't know how to change it. They knew they weren't modeling good behavior for their children. In fact, ten-year-old Devon and his eight-year-old sister Angela had learned to stay in their bedrooms when they heard mom and dad returning from a night out, having come to expect them to be stumbling and yelling at each other.

Jay and Jessica deflated as they admitted many missteps with each other and with the children. Neither of them wanted to accept personal responsibility for the difficulties. Yet, when they described the early years of their relationship, they both lit up. They were amused by their own history, and they laughed as they recalled particularly memorable episodes. They couldn't believe it was twelve years ago. From across the room, I could see them transport back to those earlier years when they looked at each other. Because the passion of youth had been such an integral part of their start, they were both having trouble letting it go. They still loved each other deeply, but that love was mired in alcohol, pot, and bad interpersonal habits. They had a lot of work to do.

THE ROAD TO RECOVERY

We started by examining the role alcohol and drugs played in their lives. Because they had never encountered legal problems, and they were high wage earners (no pun intended) living a comfortable upper-middle class lifestyle, it just didn't occur to them that their recreational use was a problem. It's not like they partied every night, like in college. Sometimes, it was only once or twice a week. Except in the summer, when the pool was open, then of course, it was more often ... and while on vacation, because, you know, they didn't have to go to work ... and at family functions, obviously, because, you know, who'd want to attend *those* sober. Jay was the first to admit there was in fact a problem. And he was reluctant but willing to name it:

"Jessica gets too emotional when she's drunk."

Luckily, Jessica was there to call out Jay's problems, too. So started a fight I was able to witness firsthand, in the here-and-now of the session.

Watching an argument unfold from the first shot fired to the final "F YOU!" is very eye-opening, and therapists will allow it, at least one time, as long as it's not too destructive, in order to see the couple's patterns emerge. Watching Jay and Jessica, certain realities about their relationship became clear. First, they wanted to hurt each other's feelings, and they didn't hesitate to use all the ammunition in their arsenal to do it. They dumped everything into this fight, including the kitchen sink (really, they brought up a home improvement project from six years prior). They swore and called each other names. The battle was a draw. They shifted to opposite ends of the couch and turned away from each other.

It had been a pretty quick exchange, no more than five minutes, and we spent exponentially more time processing it, discovering the issues beneath the anger. That's when the tears began to flow. There was such sadness between them, but they could never get there because the anger overpowered the interactions. In this calmer, more humbled state, they could finally talk about their substance use and abuse, their verbal and emotional abusiveness towards each other, and the future they wanted for their family. Once they had a shared vision, the rest of our sessions together were very productive, as we worked toward bringing that vision into their lives.

Love Will Keep Us Together was a mantra that carried Jay and Jessica through their first fifteen years together. It masked destructive patterns and thwarted their change process until their children were old enough to hold up a mirror for them. With intense therapy and total commitment, they were able to change their patterns. Part of that change involved letting go of old resentments and rage.

The rage that Jay and Jessica felt is not uncommon among couples who have gotten into destructive habits. Meet Connor and Elaine. They came in for counseling in agreement that Elaine got "too crazy" during their fights, which scared them both. He was uncertain of his own safety and that of the children, and she agreed that when she "got like that" she was out of control. Still, they loved each other, and they were determined to make this relationship work.

Connor and Elaine: Understanding Rage

Connor and Elaine had five children and a traditional division of responsibilities. He worked hard as a project manager while she raised the children. He often came home in the evening to find dirty dishes in the sink but no dinner for him. He frequently found Elaine flopped on the couch, which angered him. She would then get defensive about how she spent her day. After all, their five children, all under age ten, were fed, safe, and scattered throughout the house doing homework, playing video games, or asleep. Still, Connor was livid that his entrance went unnoticed and unappreciated: no dinner, a dirty house, an unresponsive wife. Elaine couldn't believe he would begrudge her a little R & R after her exhausting day. "What's so hard?" he asked on one particular occasion. "That's ALL you have to do!" She retorted, "You want me to baby you like you're a child! Grow up and get over it!" He continued to dig in, and she "lost it," letting loose a tirade of swears and insults, pounding around the room with fists clenched. She described it as an almost out of body experience. She could hear herself, but she had no way of stopping it. The fight ended when she stormed off to the bedroom and slammed the door. He rolled up his sleeves and went into the kitchen to tackle the mess.

THE FIGHT OR FLIGHT RESPONSE

Before we process their pattern, let's consider the human brain in three parts. The oldest part is referred to as the *mammalian* brain because it's the part of the brain we share with all other mammals. It controls our survival functions (e.g., breathing and heart rate), and when under threat, it lights up with activity as we try to cope, draining resources from other parts of the brain. Next, consider the *neocortex* — the crinkly-looking grey matter that sits just under the skull and houses all of our best and most human attributes — which distinguishes us from other animals. Here we find our sense of humor, ability to problem solve and reason, think creatively, and formulate new ideas and insights. This is the "H.O.T." brain, because it is where this **H**igher **O**rder **T**hinking resides. So we've got the oldest and newest parts of the brain, and they are connected by the part in the middle, called *working memory* because it's the part that holds current thoughts, both what we pull in from our external world and what we pull down from long-term storage. Each part plays an important role when we are under stress.

Let's review Connor and Elaine's stories one at a time, using what we know about the brain to understand their experiences.

CONNOR'S STORY

Connor works very hard under a lot of pressure to provide for his wife and five children. It is important to him that his wife stay home to raise their young family. He is a can-do man with energy to get things done, and if he's feeling tired, he just digs deeper and wills his way through it. When he is home, he is on family duty. He doesn't mind cleaning up after dinner, helping the kids with homework, or getting them to bed. He grew up believing you work until the day is done, period. When he arrives home after work, he can't wait to see his kids and find out what they've been up to all day. He wants to be appreciated for the hard work he does on their behalf, and that includes a greeting at the door and dinner on the table. When he walks in and no one notices, he feels unimportant. When he sees dinner is over, he is hurt no one waited to eat with him. When he sees the kitchen is a mess, he feels neglected that no one bothered to clean up for him. And when he sees Elaine on the couch, he feels abandoned because she doesn't care enough about him to get up and greet him.

His feeling words — *unimportant, hurt, neglected,* and *abandoned* — are important, but even more so, notice how his interpretation of events casts him as the victim in each scenario. Everyone else's behavior is about *him,* and he ends up on the short end of the stick. It couldn't be that Elaine is exhausted from meeting the demands of children all day long; it's that she doesn't *care* enough about him to find more energy to greet him. Once he is cast as *victim* in this way, his brain detects a threat and the old mammalian brain takes over to defend against it. By personalizing the actions of others in his home, making them about him and seeing himself as the victim, he triggers his own defenses and prepares for battle. His heart pounds, breathing shallows, and his eyes narrow. He is ready for a fight. His brain's resources drain from his H.O.T. brain to cope, so he is unable to use humor or appreciate the scene from anyone else's perspective in that moment.

ELAINE'S STORY

Having spent her day in high gear, caring for children and running the house, by 6 p.m. Elaine is physically exhausted and mentally drained. Flopped on the couch, she begins to construct a mental list of tasks she didn't have time for and sketches out the next day's agenda. Although she had felt pretty good about her day's accomplishments, as the neglected items start piling up in her head, she begins to feel more and more like a failure. She suddenly feels the weight of her body as she sinks into the couch. She hasn't yet lost the last ten pounds of baby weight from her most recent pregnancy, and she misses her old body and wonders if she'll ever feel like herself again. When Connor comes home and gets angry with her, Elaine experiences his criticism as a threat and she immediately gets defensive. She tries to justify her exhaustion, explaining the variety of demands placed on her all day long. He fails to see what could be so tiring and continues his criticism. Feeling like she couldn't possibly have done any more or any better, she starts to get really upset. She needs nurturing and support, and when she doesn't get it, her angst turns to overwhelm. Her identity centers around her roles of wife and mother, and in this moment, she feels like a failure at both. As Connor holds up a mirror to these feelings by criticizing her, it feels like he is rubbing her nose in it, which turns her overwhelm to a tidal wave of rage. Her brain's resources flood the old mammalian part of her brain, such that her physiological response prepares her for battle — heart pounding, sweating, all the major muscle groups keyed up and ready for action. Simultaneously, her H.O.T. brain, the brain that could help her in this moment, is effectively shut down. With all of the brain's resources allocated elsewhere, she can't use any of her advanced thinking skills to cope in that moment. In a sense, her best self *disconnects from her body.*

As we processed their stories in session, Conner could see immediately how his interpretation of others' behaviors contributed to his anger. He realized his own thought process was setting him up for failure on a daily basis. Eventually, he accepted that real life was not going to look like a 1960s television show; however, he also realized that everyone in the family (himself included) needed to work on expressing gratitude for each other. He was going to take a lead role in that. When Elaine understood this explanation for her "crazy" reaction, it changed *everything* for her. It was as though a mystery had been solved. She was overcome with joy, because she knew that if she could understand it, she could learn to control it. She had a new way of appreciating the connection between her mind and body, and she committed to taking advantage of this new awareness.

They both realized they could use their own working memory to reactivate their H.O.T. brains, thus reengaging self-regulation skills that were lost when they triggered each other. Learning some basic grounding techniques helped them in two ways: First, they were immediately better equipped to cope more effectively in the stressful moments. When they experienced strong and painful emotions, they could step away from the situation and utilize grounding tools to thwart a ramp up to a major blow out. Second, by practicing these techniques frequently, they each got in touch with their body's energy. Once they knew what *grounded* felt like, they were better at sensing when they were getting pulled off their center, and thus able to sidestep many fights before they even began. Here are the basic grounding skills we worked on together:

(1) Breathing. With one hand on your chest and the other on your belly, slowly inhale while counting to three. When you come to the "top" of the breath, slow down and pause for a moment, and then make an "O" with your lips and allow the air to press out on the exhale while slowly counting to three. Allow all of the air to totally empty out as you reach the "bottom" of the breath. You are in no rush to begin the next breath. Let your body decide when *it* is ready. Repeat. Feel the air fill up your belly before it gets to your lungs. As you exhale, feel the points of tension in your body drop, as you sink into a relaxed state. Let your body set the pace of each breath. Don't rush it at either end. Trust that your body knows what to do. When you exhale, really let it go. This is the deep breathing your body does when you are asleep and your conscious mind is off the clock. In this exercise, you are trying to get your mind out of your body's way as it does what it knows how to do naturally!

(2) Distraction. Wiggle your toes on one foot and then press them against the floor. Roll your foot down until your heal is pressed against the floor. Repeat with the other foot. Stand on both feet and be mindful of your center of gravity, distributing your weight equally on both sides and balancing toe-to-heal. Take a deep breath and as you exhale, feel yourself connecting to the floor through the soles of your feet. Drop your shoulders. Relax.

(3) Self-talk. *"I am very angry right now but I know it will pass. I am going to stay calm in this moment."* Count to ten. Even if you have an angry voice, it is okay to speak. Hear your voice and be mindful of how angry you sound. How does it sound to you? Be aware it is not a voice you prefer. Identify it as an angry voice, and then talk yourself down to a more soothing voice. *"Just because I am angry, doesn't mean I'm going to speak with this terrible voice!"* Take a deep breath. You are simultaneously giving yourself feedback about what you are hearing while you distract yourself from the source of your anger. *"It's going to be okay. I need to be my best self in this moment."*

I recommend everyone learn and practice some basic grounding skills. Regular practice is important so that the skills will be an integrated part of your repertoire and therefore accessible under stress, when you need them the most. You need to tune into your body and what "relaxed" *feels* like. The more cognizant you are about how you want to feel, the more clear it will be to you at the first sign that something is pulling you off this centered and grounded place.

Each of these techniques allows the whole brain to reengage in the scene. They divert the brain's activity away from the old mammalian brain and reactivate the H.O.T. brain. Just this information alone was a godsend for Elaine, who was so relieved to hear she was not crazy. She did have the power to control herself in those moments, she just hadn't learned to use her body's natural resources. She began to be more objective about how she wanted to react and why. With her emotions under control, she was able to have more fruitful conversations about the demands of parenting five young children alone all day long. She reengaged in conversations with her husband from a position of strength.

The ability to self-regulate is required in order to keep aggressive emotions from turning into volatile and dangerous behavior. Everything we need is in the brain, we just don't always know how to use the gift of self-regulation. Understanding how it all works helps some people find the courage and motivation to try.

CONCLUSION

As Cinderella put it, *"So this is love."* Love won't always keep you together with your partner, nor should it. By understanding the different kinds of love we get when various components are present, absent, healthy, or unhealthy, we have a better idea of what's wrong and how it can be fixed. At the same time, it helps us to understand the importance of being a healthy, whole person first, before coupling with another. If you and your partner are in a relationship because you love each other, think of that as the starting point and not the end point. Love shouldn't keep in you in a destructive relationship, but it can provide you the motivation to become your best self in order to make the relationship work.

MYTH 8:
I MARRIED THE PERFECT PERSON

Let's cut to the chase. "Perfect person" is an oxymoron. There is no such thing as a perfect person, nor could there be. Common definitions of *perfect* include *conforming to an ideal type, complete beyond practical or theoretical improvement,* and *exactly fitting a certain need.*[17] The first two descriptions imply that a *perfect person* would have neither room nor need for any other growth. This contradicts the basic principles of human development, defined as *a process of change from conception to death*. Logically, a "perfect person" is no longer subject to the laws of human development. The implication being this person is somehow in the realm of divine, and not human.

The very essence of humanity is imperfection!

The last definition, *exactly fitting a certain need*, is interesting because it trumpets *your perfection* is determined by how well you meet *my needs!* It's not about the inherent qualities of you, it's about me and my needs. That indicates a very special kind of egocentrism. Furthermore, when a spouse fails to meet my needs precisely the way I want them to be met, I may be inclined to refer to the *imperfections* as *flaws*. Let's look at that particular four-letter F-word. At its heart, *flaw* means a *defect that impairs soundness.* I suppose it's an okay word for describing the seal of an airtight container or the craftsmanship of my chair. If the *soundness* of the container or chair is *imper-*

---

[17] www.dictionary.com accessed 1/12/2011.

fect, the very purpose for which the object exists cannot be served. Air in the container will ruin the contents. A flaw in my chair may land me on the ground in a painful crash. So maybe I'm picking on the word *flaw* when I shouldn't be. It's an acceptable little F-word to describe an object that has a very specific purpose yet fails to accomplish that purpose.

I stand by my rejection if it's used to refer to the multidimensional and dynamic human condition, especially in our culture, where *flaws* demand rejection. A *flawed car* is a lemon, and there are laws to protect us from getting stuck with one of those. A *flawed argument* necessitates a losing argument. Finding the *"fatal flaw"* in academic research is the hammer that slams down to say it will never be of value sufficient for publication.

First, we must accept the reality that no one is perfect. There cannot be, nor should we want there to be, *perfection* among us mere mortals. Still, it's not uncommon to hear someone trumpet they've married the perfect person, so we need to figure out what's going on here. Somebody's not being honest, but is it "the person who married the perfect person" or the "perfect person" the someone married? This myth is among the more inherently destructive to genuine intimacy because somebody's not being honest.

GAMES PEOPLE PLAY

Are you the spouse claiming to be married to the perfect person? If so, are you a *believer* or a *manipulator?* If you are genuine in your belief that your spouse is perfect, you are trumpeting your fatuous love; you may have the passion and commitment, but you cannot truly know and cherish the *real person* that your partner is if you fail to see their human qualities. If you are being manipulative, then you are disingenuously labeling your spouse "perfect" for your own gain. After all, it would be handy to marry a *perfect* person — *none of those messy human qualities for you to put up with!*

Do you go along with your spouse's claim that *you* are perfect? If so, are *you* a *believer* or a *manipulator?* If you genuinely believe you are perfect, this could indicate a range of issues, from mild (you are well intentioned but perhaps naive) to profound (you suffer from narcissism). If you are manipulative, you may be putting up the front of perfection in order to keep your spouse deluded.

The games people play depend on who believes and who manipulates. If you both believe the myth, then you are perhaps content in your fatuous love. You are *playing house*, each going through the motions of marriage, but the *core intimacy* of really knowing each other is absent, as is the *concern* that you don't know each other better.

If neither of you believe it, but you claim it's true, you are both manipulators, and the game is *charades*. You each play your role to keep up the facade. The relationship is like a grand performance, and you each act your part.

The other two scenarios, in which one spouse is a believer and the other a manipulator, are the subjects of our case examples. In the first example, we meet Roy, who genuinely believes he is married to a perfect person, and Mandy, who knows it isn't true but happily goes along. In the second example, we meet Billy, who claims his wife is perfect in order to manipulate her, and Tammy, who is all too eager to believe it is true.

He Believes and She Manipulates: A Game of Blind Man's Bluff

Blind Man's Bluff is a children's game in which one person is blindfolded and wanders around trying to find someone hiding in plain sight. The person hiding manipulates their partner, trying to mislead him to avoid getting caught.

Roy and Mandy grew up together in the same neighborhood. She was physically very beautiful, and Roy beamed at her while he mused, "And she always has been." Her home life had not been so beautiful; her parents had married very young and spent equal time abusing each other and their children. Mandy coped as well as she could until she could no longer take it. At age seventeen, she met an older man and ran away with him. No one from the neighborhood heard from her until five years later, when she reached out to Roy for help, which he was eager to give. They reunited, eloped, and moved into a small apartment in a new city for a fresh start. He didn't ask a lot of questions about their time apart; he was so relieved she was safe and eager to focus on their future.

For the first few months, all seemed well. They both found jobs, he was in sales and she worked at a local restaurant. Her passion was singing, and waiting tables allowed her to hit open mic nights when they came up.

As they settled into their life together, Roy started getting curious about the five years they had spent apart. Mandy was very guarded and didn't want to share that with him. From her point of view, it was over and done. She had made terrible mistakes and wanted to move on with her life. As much as she loved and appreciated him, she wasn't willing to reveal her past to him. Roy was terribly hurt by this. From his perspective, they were family. He knew all about her painful childhood, having experienced it with her. He professed his unconditional love and just wanted to help her exercise whatever demons she was carrying from her past.

"Tell me what you love about your wife," I asked.

"Everything!" he replied. "She's family. I know her as well as I could know anyone. She's smart, and funny, and so kind." He was absolutely glowing as he looked at her and said, "She's just perfect."

And there it was. The minute he said it, I could feel her energy recoil. She wasn't able to respond in that moment because she was overwhelmed with emotions, though her appearance did not change. In a subsequent individual session, she unpacked all those feelings.

"He says he loves me; he doesn't even know me. Yes, we grew up together, but he wasn't in my house. He knows there was abuse, but he doesn't know what really went on."

Over the next few sessions, Mandy revealed her painful history of sexual abuse. Holographic Memory Resolution[18] helped her to process and let go of trauma she had bottled up for years. She opened up about her more recent past. At age seventeen, she had joined a cult, and getting out had been a narrow escape. How could Roy possibly understand? How could he possibly love her if he really knew her?

Working with Mandy and Roy over the course of several months involved couples sessions and individual work. Roy was wearing a blindfold, very genuine in his belief that she was perfect and deserved to be on a pedestal. Mandy knew his image of her was inaccurate, but it worked to her advantage, so she was not willing to challenge it. Because she was so lovely and calm all the time, he assumed she was happy and the marriage was strong. Meanwhile, she could quietly go

---

[18]Holographic Memory Resolution (HMR) is a therapeutic technique that resolves trauma in the mind and body, developed by Brent Baum. For more information, you can visit his website www.healingdimensions.com.

about her business, floating along like a balloon on a string. Yes, she was comfortable in the marriage, but by accepting this shallow level of intimacy, a passing breeze could have pulled the string from his hand and out of reach.

Before she could experience genuine intimacy with him, she needed to heal and love herself. This process takes time and it requires motivation. Mandy struggled to find that motivation, because her life finally felt good. She had a safe home, a secure income, and a husband who thought she was *perfect*. In reality, she was hiding in plain sight. She was not allowing her husband to know the genuine *her*. She was happy to watch shows he selected, prepare and eat dinners he liked, go out when he wanted to the places he enjoyed. She was content to float along in order to get along. In her private sessions, she was sharp-witted, a bit sarcastic, and so *real*. *"That's not who he wants to be with,"* she told me when I asked why I never see this side of her in sessions with him. We were able to get to the heart of the matter, her fear of rejection.

If he really knew me, he wouldn't love me.

It felt safer to Mandy to keep Roy blindfolded.

PERFECTION BLOCKS INTIMACY

On a very deep level, perhaps Roy suspected the intimacy problem, but he could not admit to that. Roy insisted the two get help to improve communication; specifically, he *worried* her secret past would be a wedge between them. In reality, it drove him crazy that he didn't know where she'd been all that time. His plan was to get a professional to help him cajole her into a confession. He did not know pressing this issue would reveal his own. By overemphasizing their connection, their history together, and their familial bond, he was able to dismiss the here-and-now reality that they hardly knew each other. Fear prevented him from admitting he could lose her. He had loved her since childhood, and the image he created of her all those years ago did not allow him curiosity about her *real* self. This was a major contribution to their intimacy issues. She was happy to go with the flow, allowing him to think he knew her so well, and continuing to live a very guarded life.

Recall we first mentioned *projection* in Chapter 2. When one person *projects perfection* onto another person, more is revealed about the projector than the projected upon. It is often the case that the projector harbors deep insecurities and needs to feel in control in order to feel safe. There is a superficial quality to their relationships, because what they see outweighs what's really there, which depersonalizes the object of their affection, making it almost impossible to have true intimacy. Without true intimacy, the *friendship* part of love can never live up to its potential.

The "perfect" partner is, in turn, under a lot of pressure to live up to the billing. There is something very flattering about it, and for a while anyway, she (or he) might enjoy the label. At the beginning of the relationship, it's natural to want to be as fabulous as your new partner thinks you are. As a more committed relationship emerges, partners have to reveal their *real* selves, so that their commitment is based on genuine compatibility and friendship, and not on a projected and inaccurate image.

Roy genuinely believed Mandy was perfect, and Mandy's need for a secure relationship outweighed her need for a genuine relationship. The process of therapy illuminated each person's role in the destructive pattern. In the next example of *"I Married the Perfect Person,"* we meet Billy, who uses the mantra as a means of purposefully maintaining an unhealthy and disingenuous marriage.

He Manipulates and She Believes: A Game of Liar's Dice

In Liar's Dice (also known as Call My Bluff), the object is for a player to look into the eyes of his opponent and bluff with complete confidence, so that the opponent believes he is telling the truth. Billy was very good at this game, and Tammy didn't know there was a game in play.

Tammy and Billy came in for counseling six weeks after she discovered his two-year office affair. She was just emerging from the shock and getting to the heart of her anger. He said the affair stemmed from arrogance and his belief that he deserved whatever in life he wanted. He was stunned she had discovered the affair, having convinced himself these separate lives would never cross. He could be a player by day and a devoted family man by night. He had done some research on the subject and read that many powerful men have affairs for the adrenaline rush. He was pretty sure that was the case here. He did not have any other explanation. The couple came to see me to find out if they could pull a marriage from the rubble that remained.

His patronizing attitude toward his wife was apparent in many ways. When Tammy was talking, he got into her personal space, stroked her hand or her hair, and called her by pet names. There was something very disingenuous, almost creepy about it. She talked about the betrayal, citing specific instances that were particularly painful. For example, on the day their teenage son's best friend was killed in a car accident, Billy went on a business trip. By lining up receipts and phone calls, Tammy worked out his girlfriend had joined him on that trip. As Tammy made these connections, his response dripped with condescension and false empathy. "I was awful. You all needed me and I wasn't there. I have no excuse. You have every right to be so mad," like he had the authority to give her permission to be angry!

When I asked him to tell me a little bit about their married life together, he went straight into her accolades. She handled everything. She was the perfect wife, mother, and hostess. She was always gracious and loving. She was absolute perfection. As he spoke, she sat with impeccable posture, listening attentively. Her facial expressions would change only slightly. It was clear that she had heard this before, and it was also clear that she was not going to speak until invited, so I asked her what she thought of what he'd said. "It's true. I do all of those things, or I did, anyway. And because I was doing everything so perfectly at home, he didn't have to take any responsibility at all. He could be out running around while I took care of everything."

She understood completely how destructive "perfection" had been in their marriage. It gave him the excuse to check out. And now, it produced a pressure on her to handle this crisis with the same grace and perfection as she handled everything else. Because she had always played the role of "perfect wife" for him, she didn't know how to handle all of these new, messy feelings. They were not aligned with who she thought she was. She didn't know how to ask for help from her closest friends and relatives. She lived from day to day in a haze, going through all the same motions but feeling disconnected from her body and detached from her relationships. Here he had been, traveling the world and flaunting this extramarital relationship across the globe, and she could not muster the strength to confide in her sister.

The concept of *real vs. ideal self* is important to both of the cases in this chapter. Carl Rogers, a therapist in the mid-20th century, theorized that a person's "real" self can only be expressed in the presence of positive regard. But to gain acceptance by our loved ones, we sometimes need to be, not our *real* selves, but an *ideal* version of ourselves. The gap between *who we are* and *how we allow ourselves to be seen* represents an incongruity that drives our anxieties. Let's compare Mandy and Tammy. Neither allowed her real self to live in her marriage, but the similarities end there. Mandy allowed her husband to believe she was perfect. She was arguably manipulating him and intentionally projecting an *ideal self* for him to see. In contrast, Tammy believed herself to be perfect; she internalized that message and worked hard to maintain that as a core truth in the marriage.

Clients often come into therapy to improve themselves and their relationships. If they aspire to be perfect, we need to explore when and how they established those aspirations. We also need to clarify what *perfection* looks like, what metric determines its achievement, and what pressure maintains their need for it. Rarely do people actually think about the ultimate goal. It's more likely they plod along feeling inadequate, regardless of their performance.

I believe most of us humans want to do our best, especially at things we value or judge to be important. We want to be good partners, good parents, good people. At our core, we want to be competent at what we do.

EXERCISE: PRACTICE IMPERFECTION

It may be that your drive for perfection interferes with your enjoyment of, and even your participation in, activities. If you play an instrument, you want it to sound pleasing to others. If you create art, you want it to move those who see it. If it doesn't, you likely consider the effort a failure and abandon the activity. It is important to practice imperfection. Get reacquainted with things you enjoy because you enjoy them, regardless of your skill or the appreciation of others. This is one avenue towards meeting your *real* self.

The exercise for this chapter is more of a personal challenge. Come up with examples of activities that belong under the headings "Did it but quit it" and "Never tried it." The example on the next page includes a few items in each column.

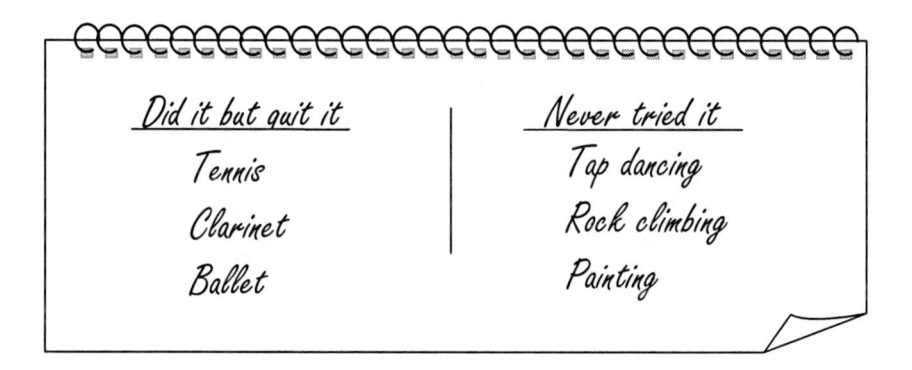

Did it but quit it	_Never tried it_
Tennis	Tap dancing
Clarinet	Rock climbing
Ballet	Painting

Your items might include sculpting, dancing, building model ships, speaking a foreign language, or playing an instrument. Look at your items in the *"Did it but quit it"* column. Why did you stop doing these activities? Was it because you were no good at them, or because you didn't enjoy them? Did you *not enjoy them* because you were not good at them? If so, how did you know you weren't good? What metric did you use, or did someone else judge you?

Now look at the items on the right, under the *"Never tried it"* heading. Why didn't you ever try these things? Was it a practical issue (time, money, opportunity), or were you afraid to try them?

Your personal challenge is to pick one activity from each list and add them to your life for at least a month, not because you're going to be good at them or earn a living doing them. If you think you will enjoy them, make time for them, no matter what your skill level. *If it's worth doing, it's worth doing poorly — if you enjoy it!* Trade in your need for perfection for your need to engage in things you enjoy.

CONCLUSION

Perfect person is an oxymoron. The myth, *I Married the Perfect Person,* is inherently destructive to a marriage because it necessitates dishonesty. It's hard to know which is worse, wanting to be perfect, or wanting to be married to a perfect person. Both are riddled with issues that affect the long-term health of the relationship. Practice imperfection and embrace it in the ones you love. *You will all be the better for it.*

MYTH 9:
SHE KNOWS ME
BETTER THAN I KNOW MYSELF

Lifelong partnership requires a certain amount of *surrender*. Yielding power to one another, in careful balance, with transparent motives and strong communication, is a prerequisite to happiness. You have to trust that your partner will not abuse this power, and you have to be diligent not to abuse the power your partner extends to you. Knowing, liking, and trusting each other make this balance of power much easier to achieve. Perhaps that feeds our motivation to *be known* by our partners. I am not advocating anything contrary to *being known,* but I still ask the question:

Why would anyone know you better than you know yourself?

GET CURIOUS ABOUT YOUR *SELF*

Are you curious about why you behave as you do? Do you wonder about events in your childhood, and how they shaped your thoughts, feelings, and behaviors along the way? And how, in turn, those thoughts, feelings, and behaviors link to your current life choices, actions, and reactions? Sometimes the connection is obvious. I will give a personal example. I prefer powdered whitener in my coffee. I don't care if it's bad for my health. I wouldn't care if it were hydrogenated oil wrapped in chemicals fried in saturated fat. It's what I will always choose. Why, when I make so many healthy choices in so many other areas, am I so stuck on this particular choice? When I was a child, the youngest of six spaced over eight years, my grandmother had a small apartment in our house. Many mornings, I escaped the chaos of my siblings to join her for coffee. In my cup, she started with a tiny bit of instant coffee, dissolved it with boiling water, and filled the rest with milk. Then came the good stuff, powdered Cremora®. I poured it in by the spoonfuls and swirled it around as we sat quietly and visited. I loved when it clumped on the surface because then I would scoop it up and eat it. To this day, Cremora® takes me right back to those special mornings with my grandmother. It's comfort food.

Admittedly, how a person prefers coffee may not be a key element to her disposition, but this serves as an example of how our likes and dislikes are shaped. Why do you prefer blue to red? Polka dots to stripes? Arguing instead of backing down? Recall our discussion about personality development in Chapter 1. A great deal of how we live day to day is linked to our experiences. I challenge you to explore who you are and how you came to be. *Be curious about your journey!*

If you believe your partner knows you better than you know yourself, I wonder if it *is* true or *what you believe* to be true. I wonder about your motivation to maintain it as true (actually or believed). If it is *actually* true, and your partner knows you better than you know yourself, I wonder what happened that made you turn your back on the most fascinating longitudinal study of your life: YOU! Did you learn that exploration of the *self* is bad, perhaps equated with pride and deemed sinful? Were you too busy minding the business of others to mind your own? Were you taught to spend so much energy on what you were doing that you skipped exploring who you were being and why? Were you judged on *how you were affecting others* regardless of your own inner wellness?

If it isn't true, he *doesn't* really know you better than you know yourself, but you believe it is, ask yourself why. What purpose is served by believing *he knows me better than I know myself?* In cases of domestic abuse, familiarity is often used as a device to keep the victim stuck. The abuser uses the message that *no one else could ever know and love you as much as I do* as a way to disempower her.[19] It drains her motivation to change the circumstance and break the pattern. Because part of our humanity includes blind spots to aspects of

---

[19]Approximately 85% of victims of domestic abuse are women, and 15% are men.

our *selves*, perhaps surrendering your knowledge of self seems *easier* than the messy process of self-discovery. Either way, it is still destructive to believe that a couple can have long-term happiness that enriches *both* if one is willing to yield their knowledge of *self* to the other or fails to be curious about their own *self*. Hence, the inclusion of this tendency in our exploration of myths that destroy *happily ever after*.

Consider if any of the following sounds like you or your spouse:

"Oh, just order me anything."
"I don't care what we do tonight."
"That sounds good! I'll have what she's having."

In some ways, these examples call to mind Mandy from Chapter 7, wanting to seem easy and agreeable in order to appear perfect. However, this is different in that the person isn't *hiding* him *self* for effect, rather, he really doesn't have a personal preference. For those of you in a marriage marked by strong wills and arguments, you might think, "I WISH!" It may even be hard to see this as a problem, but like any personal quality, there is a healthy dose and an extreme. *Easygoing* and *flexible* are certainly desirable characteristics, but *indifferent* and *wishy-washy* take those characteristics to a level that will cause problems for both self and relationships. Asserting your *self* in your relationship requires that you know your *self* and you are empowered to express what you know.

To be clear, I do not advocate holding back from your spouse or being someone you are not. You deserve a spouse who knows you completely, loves you totally, and commits to the relationship fully. (Your spouse deserves the same.) I am talking about your knowledge of *self* and your willingness to own what you know.

Your partner shouldn't know you *less*.
You should know yourself *more!*

FIND YOUR TRUTH

Getting to know your *self* includes both personal preferences (interests and tastes) and the more enduring personality characteristics we addressed in Chapter 1. Assertiveness, extraversion, stubbornness, and kindness, for example, are qualities we express to varying degrees based on circumstance. Digging into *who you are* will help you reveal your truth and perhaps help you to avoid the "blame game" I hear many clients play. Scott was a typical example.

Scott's Blame: Better Out than In
Scott came in for help, discontented with his life. He had many blessings — a successful job, healthy children, a loving wife. Still, something was missing. He was getting bored and dabbling in potentially destructive behaviors, such as gambling, drinking, and spending time with single friends. He considered having an affair. Rather than looking inward for his source of discontent, he looked outward. The person who always seemed to be in the picture was his wife, so he began to convince himself she must be the source of the problem.

Too often, we reach a point of discontentment in our lives and avoid personal responsibility for it by looking to our spouse as the "cause."

"I'm not happy, but if you would just _____, then I would be."

Just like Nadine in Chapter 3, this is another example of the myth *"If you would be perfect, I could be happy."* It's often years later, after they've exhausted all external possibilities (and gone through a number of marriages and vices in the process) that people like Scott awaken to the possibility that they had the answers within all along. *They just hadn't bothered to get to know themselves.*

First, you must find your truth. This is no small task as our defenses work overtime to protect us from many things that are true but unflattering or undesirable (e.g., think of Nadine's issues from Chapter 3). It might help to find a non-threatening example of your vice-in-action as a way of exploring your *self* without triggering the defenses along the perimeter. Let's try to sneak up on our truths using the cast of *Gilligan's Island*.

To which character (or characters) can you relate? Are you lustful, like Ginger, or envious, like Mary Ann? Do you rage like the Skipper, or are you prideful, like the Professor? Are you greedy like

Mr. Howell, or gluttonous like Mrs. Howell? Or are you just plain lazy, like Gilligan? I love using these archetypes as a touchstone, because they're so over the top that your milder version of the vice may not seem so bad. If *Gilligan's Island* wasn't your show, pick other characters from other shows you can relate to. Whether it's Mrs. Kravitz from *Bewitched*, or Mrs. McCluskey from *Desperate Housewives*, if your vice is nosing into the business of others, that's your *truth* and it's time to own it.

Once you identify your truth, you can take a big deep breath, close your eyes, and decide if it is a truth you embrace or one that no longer serves you. Only *you* can decide what to do with your truths, once revealed.

EXERCISE

This exercise might help you gain some insights about your *truth*. Start by identifying a current struggle in your life or daily routine. Do so by completing the following sentence with ten words or fewer. Your answer can represent a big thing (e.g., going to work every day, my teenage daughter's new boyfriend) or small (e.g., showing my toes at the pool, weird people who sit with me on the train).

I struggle with_____.

Now do it ten more times, writing out your answers as you go. Many people find it difficult to complete the sentence the first few times, but it gets easier with practice, so by the tenth sentence, they have a few more they can tack on. Go ahead! It's all about you.

Once you have your list of struggles, look through it and find the links. What do the struggles have in common? Are they matters of interpersonal relationships, daily routines, or personal self-efficacy? Do they identify a tendency to struggle with what you do or with *others* for what they do? Consider why you find these matters a struggle. Do you have unmet expectations for other people's behavior? Could it be that your expectations are too high, or do they reveal a desire to be at the center of another person's world? What do you expect from yourself and others, and how do you judge failings? All of this can be important to understand as you seek your truth, and so it is important information for you to access. That is why:

You have to be curious about your *self* and your motives.

Once you have better insight into why you feel the way you feel under different circumstances, you can take a more active role in being safe, balanced, and grounded throughout your day.

Leticia and Jillian: A Truth Revealed
Leticia gave up her job in advertising to raise her three children. Her oldest, Jillian, was in the sixth grade. Leticia came in for therapy feeling overwhelmed and anxious. Among her issues was growing anxiety over Jillian's middle school experience. Jillian had to work hard to achieve B grades. Her passion was horseback riding, and she preferred the barn to the mall and the horses to the kids in her school. The struggles Leticia identified through the exercise were all about her daughter.

- *I struggle with Jillian not being popular, and what that will mean to her.*
- *I struggle with what the other kids are saying about her behind her back.*
- *I struggle with how the other moms treat her.*
- *I struggle with what they say to their daughters about her.*
- *I struggle with her being lonely and isolating herself from everybody.*

"What's the connection here? How can we understand these together?" I wondered aloud.

"Well, clearly it's all about Jillian. She's a social outcast and she has no idea the heartache that's ahead of her," Leticia replied.

"How is she doing with all of this?"

"Oh, she doesn't care," Leticia responded through her tears. Exasperated, she erupted, "She doesn't get it at all!"

As the conversation continued with Leticia, it became clear that Jillian was aware of the social politics at her middle school, she just did not care. Leticia, on the other hand, couldn't imagine her daughter escaping the pain of the "Queen Bees" and "Wanna Bees." She *was constantly trying to orchestrate friendships, and chastising Jillian for not getting more involved. I suggested the possibility of a third group, the "Don't Cares," and that "Queen Bees" could only hurt the "Wanna Bees." They can't hurt the "Don't Cares" because those girls are out of reach. This simple idea was a revelation for Leticia. As she examined the history of events as they had unfolded, she realized that her anxiety began as the school year approached, knowing that Jillian was to start middle school. On the first day, at the morning drop off, Leticia saw women talking and laughing together, which she interpreted as cliquey moms gossiping. This triggered painful memories of her experience as a social outsider in middle school. Leticia, who had been a "Wanna Bee," was projecting her own traumatic middle school experience onto Jillian. As a grown, successful woman, she never imagined the trauma of those years was still lurking in her subconscious, waiting for a chance to pounce. By exploring and understanding this, we were able to focus therapy where it needed to be, not on Jillian, who by all accounts was fine, but on Leticia's painful experiences with bullying at the hands of her peers. By understanding herself, she cleared out her pain and enjoyed a more peaceful relationship with Jillian.*

THE GIFT OF *KNOWING* IN RELATIONSHIP

Knowing and *being known* are the most precious gifts in any relationship. The best case scenario looks like this:

"He knows me almost as well as I know myself, adores me, and embraces my humanity. Likewise, I know him almost as well as he knows himself, adore him, and embrace his humanity."

Think about the beauty that can exist between two people when this is true. It has to do with knowledge of self and other. Maybe that's why the start of a relationship *feels* so good. Most of us come into adulthood baring the scars of adolescence. Healing our *selves* in the aftermath of our own immaturity, and all the painful lessons we endured to reach adulthood, can be very difficult. When we meet someone new, someone unencumbered by our past, we get to enjoy who we've become without tripping over who we were. The gift is really the open acceptance, void of judgment or criticism. Once the relationship has its own history, with ups and downs, moments of great joy and regrettable pain, there is opportunity for judgment and criticism to creep in. The tendency to find fault in your partner likely stems from your old wounds. Your relationship will be tested. Now that you've gotten to know each other's *real* selves, can you fully embrace one another with open hearts and unencumbered acceptance?

Can you love the humanness of your partner, or do you harbor secret hopes that he has superhuman abilities to read your mind, solve your problems, and fold the perfect shirt? Couples get into knots when they start testing each other. They set each other up for failure, then follow up with criticism because they "should" have ... known, done, said, etc. It's not always about the big ticket items, either. A whole bunch of smaller-ticket items will eventually accumulate into the same expensive burden. Here's an example of a very minor event that may seem hardly worth mentioning at first glance.

Jack and Jane: I'll Have What He's Having
Jack and Jane brought their kids to a family restaurant, and as was their routine, Jack slid into the booth while Jane directed the children to follow her to the bathroom to wash hands.

"If the server comes for drinks before you get back, what can I order for you?" Jack asked.

Jane replied, "Just get me anything."

En route from the bathroom, Jane saw another patron's milkshake and it looked very delicious. She thought to herself, "Ooh, I hope Jack surprises me with a milkshake!" Jane was disappointed when her iced tea arrived.

"What's wrong?" asked Jack.

"Nothing, it's fine," she replied, feeling a little let down.

Jane set herself (and Jack) up for failure. If she had a preference, she should have said so, and she should have spoken up for herself instead of waiting to see if Jack would get it right. Jack is not a mind reader. What if he had guessed *milkshake* but that wasn't the right answer? Jane might have gotten upset. *"Doesn't he know I'm trying to lose weight?"* This is the ultimate no win for him. Jane is testing him to see if he knows what's in her mind (even before she knows). What was an opportunity for her to express a preference for herself ended up being Jack's failure. When we debriefed the situation in session, it was clearly not about the milkshake. Jane wanted to be cared for, loved, and *known*. As a child, Jane's dad always seemed to know just what would make her happy on special occasions. He surprised her on birthdays with special gifts. Now she put Jack into the role of parent, wanting him to carry on this tradition. Recall the key question from Chapter 2 that helps us to pinpoint when we learned unhelpful thinking, patterns, or expectations. For Jane, the question was this:

> *"How old might I be when I first learn to equate surprise gestures with feeling known and loved?"*

Her answer was, "About six." It's time for Jane to let go of this old way of thinking that no longer serves her and step into her *adult* self, capable of loving herself and meeting her own needs. In this new paradigm, any surprises from Jack will be just that — surprises. Receiving them will be a true gift, rather than the fulfillment of an unfair expectation.

So, the desire to be *known and loved* could link back to childhood in this way.

LEARNING TO DOUBT YOUR *SELF*

There are two other noteworthy manifestations of the *He Knows Me Better Than I Know Myself* myth, each very different from the other. On one hand, you can have someone who is just plain intrapersonally[20] lazy. These people are content to muddle through life unexamined. They float along unwilling to change. Life isn't turning out as they wanted, but they're not willing to try to live any other way. Scott was like that. He didn't want to bother exploring himself. It was easier to blame others for his unhappiness.

On the other hand, a person may be unable to make a decision because of a deep-seated fear about making decisions. Where might *that* come from? Let's look at exchanges between a mother and her daughter, Jenny, at different points in Jenny's childhood:

---

[20] The term *intrapersonal* refers to what is going on within one person. *Interpersonal* means how people interact with each other. So, *intrapersonal awareness* refers to how well you understand yourself, and *interpersonal awareness* refers to how well you understand social dynamics between two or more people.

> **Mom:** *Which one do you want?*
> **Six-year-old Jenny:** *I want the pink one.*
> **Mom:** *It doesn't match the pants. Take the green.*

Six-year-old Jenny had a preference, which turned out to be "wrong." Mom was there to show her the error in her judgment and help her know the "right" preference.

> **Mom:** *What do you want for lunch?*
> **Twelve-year-old Jenny:** *I want pepperoni pizza.*
> **Mom:** *Oh, honey, you know that's fattening and bad for your skin. I think you should have a salad.*

Not only did twelve-year-old Jenny pick the "wrong" option, but mom *should-ed* on her, always an invitation to feel shameful. Additionally, it is a shame-inducing "wrong" choice *involving food,* surely fueling the fire of body image and weight-related issues experienced by so many adolescents.

> **Mom:** *What are you going to do tonight?*
> **Sixteen-year-old Jenny:** *We're just going to watch a movie over at Brenda's house.*
> **Mom:** *Okay, honey. Have fun. Call if you need a ride!*

No expressed conflict here; it's just not true. The truth is that sixteen-year-old Jenny and Brenda are going to a party with boys. If there is a "right answer" and an "answer that induces shame, guilt, or fear," you're going to get the "right answer" every time. It may not be the truthful answer, but that's operant conditioning[21] for you.

If you grow up unable to trust that the choices you make — big or small — are ever the "right" choices, then you will likely have an issue trusting yourself and your decisions. Either you will learn to be deceitful to avoid contradiction and conflict, or you will actually lose

---

[21] *Operant Conditioning* is a theory about how we learn. Behaviors that are punished decrease and behaviors that are reinforced are increased. I addressed the concept in Chapter 1, but this is the academic label for that kind of learning.

touch with your self and what you really prefer, as was the case with one client of mine.

In session, this client admitted to me, *"I was never allowed to make up my own mind when I was growing up — EVER!"* As an adult, she gladly allowed her husband to make big decisions and she had a host of issues around food. She could only eat a narrow range of choices, the food had to be prepared a certain way, and she could only eat under certain conditions. This made functioning in the real world a struggle. She traced back her anxiety and fears to *never being right* about personal choices in her childhood. She had learned to believe that she was incapable of making good choices, and as a result, she *freaked out* (her words) when presented with choices. Hiding behind her husband's decisions was one successful coping strategy. Carefully controlling food was another. Unfortunately, such strategies couldn't prevent her anxiety from slipping out in other ways. She had difficulty sleeping at night. She was a trained and beautiful dancer, but she worked in a meaningless job, afraid to depend on her talents for a living. Her therapeutic goal was to discover her *self* and live her *truth*.

COMMUNICATING ABOUT FEELINGS EFFECTIVELY (CAFE)

One issue common to couples in therapy is communication. Interestingly, not all communication difficulties are created equal. Sometimes couples don't have time to communicate; sometimes it's motivation they lack. In the context of this myth, communication problems can stem from one partner's fears about the consequences of honesty. This could be a result of experience. If every time you mention your discontent, your spouse gets angry, you will learn to defer to your spouse and keep your discontentment to yourself. This tendency could also be the result of growing up in a home in which your thoughts were mocked or simply dismissed as unimportant. It is likely a *learned behavior* is driving your communication issues, and it's time to *unlearn* it.

Many traditional communication exercises are based on the premise that *my partner has to understand me.* One in particular I have never understood looks like this: One partner (let's say, the wife) speaks, uninterrupted, for five minutes, and then the other partner has to respond, saying what he heard. Then it's his turn to speak for five minutes, and she has to reflect on what he said.

As the exercise stands, it feeds into the *"He knows me better than I know myself"* myth. *"I can blab on for five minutes and the burden is on him to figure out what I've said without further pissing me off."* The most important piece of communication is missing: the preparation, when the sender of the message works to understand their own message before sending it out for delivery to another. I developed a communication tool in my practice that addresses this shortcoming, and I call it the CAFE exercise.

COMMUNICATE ABOUT FEELINGS EFFECTIVELY (CAFE)

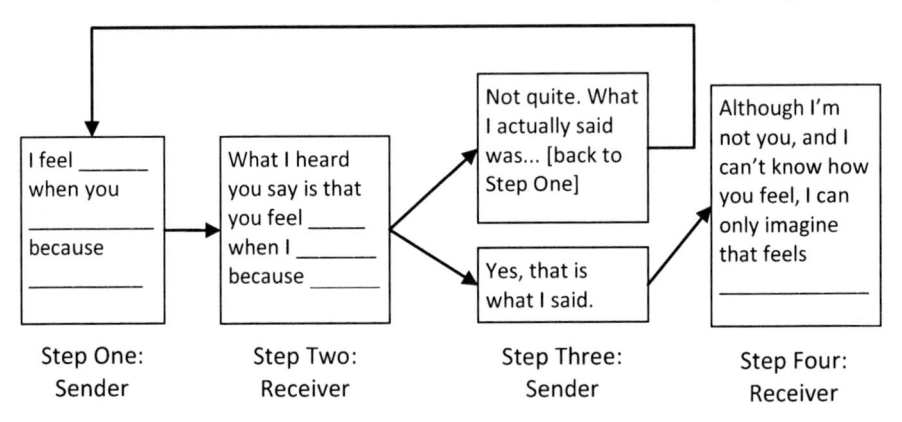

Step One: Sender	Step Two: Receiver	Step Three: Sender	Step Four: Receiver
I feel ____ when you ____ because ____	What I heard you say is that you feel ____ when I ____ because ____	Not quite. What I actually said was... [back to Step One] / Yes, that is what I said.	Although I'm not you, and I can't know how you feel, I can only imagine that feels ____

CAFE: THE KEYS FOR SUCCESS AT EACH STEP

STEP ONE. The burden is really for you, as the sender of the message, to get your head clear before trying to communicate with your partner. This is about understanding and taking personal responsibility for your feelings. Thoughtfully identify how you feel and be precise. *Angry, frustrated,* and *unheard* are each important feelings to process, but they also have unique root causes. Run the dialogue three times if you are feeling all three, but don't try to address more than one feeling at a time. Also be sure that the "because" is followed by an explanation of the feeling and not just a pile on related to the offense.

Here's an example of one client's first attempt at Step One.

"I feel really pissed off that you didn't call me because you should call me during the day."

There are two big problems with this feeling statement. First, "pissed off" is not precise enough to be helpful. According to www.thesaurus.com,[22] there are 38 synonyms for the expression "pissed off," many of which would offer a more precise account of the feeling.

Second, the "because" is linked to the listener's behavior, not the sender's feeling. *"You should call me"* does not account for the sender's feelings, but *"I believe I am entitled to communication from you,"* does.

When I am working with clients to help them learn this process, I provide them with a list of words to help them to be more precise in understanding and expressing their emotions. You will find the list on the next page. The client from the example above looked over this list to find a more precise way to express her anger. She chose "provoked," and then continued to scan the list for other words to capture her feelings. In so doing, she realized she was feeling so much more than just pissed off. She felt *hurt* and *alarmed.*

Her work was not done. She still had to figure out where those feelings were coming from within her. People are naturally inclined to attribute their bad feelings directly to the other person's behavior. *"I'm angry because you should have called."* In reality, that behavior does not inherently evoke a particular emotion. There are lots of people he didn't call during the course of the day, and most of them have no emotional response. Likewise, she knows lots of people who didn't call her, but she's not mad at them. We cannot say anything inherent in the act of "not calling" is solely responsible for triggering anger. The purpose of this exercise is to unpack and understand the part you can own, **your** emotional response. *What was it about him not calling you that upset you so much?*

---

[22] www.thesaurus.com accessed 11/6/2010. Synonyms of *pissed off* were listed as: affronted, annoyed, bent out of shape, boiling, cross, displeased, enraged, fighting mad, fit to be tied, fuming, furious, hopping mad, hot, huffy, in a tizzy, incensed, inflamed, infuriated, irate, irritated, livid, mad, maddened, offended, outraged, peed, peeved off, provoked, raging, riled, sore, steamed, steamed up, steaming, storming, t'd off, tee'd off, ticked off.

Feeling Words

AFRAID	ANGRY	CONFUSED	DEPRESSED	HURT	INADEQUATE	LONELY	SORRY
Alarmed	Aggravated	Ambivalent	Awful	Abused	Ailing	Abandoned	Apologetic
Anxious	Annoyed	Baffled	Beaten down	Achy	Blemished	Alienated	Ashamed
Apprehensive	Belligerent	Bewildered	Blah	Belittled	Broken	Alone	Bashful
Cautious	Bitter	Chaotic	Bleak	Cheapened	Crippled	Apart	Chagrined
Defensive	Crabby	Disorganized	Blue	Crushed	Damaged	Blue	Contrite
Distressed	Cranky	Distracted	Dejected	Damaged	Defeated	Cut-off	Disgraced
Fearful	Dismayed	Dizzy	Demoralized	Degraded	Deficient	Dejected	Embarrassed
Fidgety	Enraged	Flustered	Devalued	Destroyed	Desperate	Deserted	Evil
Fretful	Exasperated	Foggy	Disappointed	Devalued	Feeble	Despondent	Exposed
Frightened	Fuming	Frustrated	Discouraged	Devastated	Flawed	Detached	Flustered
Horrified	Furious	Mistaken	Dispirited	Discredited	Helpless	Discouraged	Guilty
Intimidated	Grouchy	Mixed-up	Distressed	Disgraced	Humiliated	Discarded	Humble
Nervous	Heated	Perplexed	Down	Distressed	Impaired	Distant	Humiliated
Panicky	Hostile	Puzzled	Empty	Forsaken	Incapable	Empty	Meek
Paralyzed	Ill-tempered	Rattled	Gloomy	Injured	Incompetent	Estranged	Mortified
Scared	Incensed	Reeling	Grief	Let down	Ineffective	Excluded	Penitent
Shaky	Indignant	Shocked	Grim	Miffed	Inept	Forsaken	Regretful
Shocked	Infuriated	Shook up	Hopeless	Minimized	Inferior	Insulated	Reluctant
Shy	Irate	Speechless	Lost	Misled	Insignificant	Isolated	Remorseful
Tense	Irked	Startled	Melancholy	Mistreated	Invalid	Left out	Repentant
Terrified	Irritated	Stumped	Miserable	Mocked	Overwhelmed	Melancholy	Sheepish
Threatened	Offended	Stunned	Moody	Neglected	Powerless	Neglected	Sinful
Timid	Outraged	Thrown	Morose	Punished	Small	Ostracized	Sorrowful
Troubled	Provoked	Troubled	Regretful	Put down	Spineless	Outcast	Sorry
Uneasy	Resentful	Uncertain	Somber	Ridiculed	Substandard	Rejected	Wicked
Unsure	Seething	Undecided	Sorrowful	Scorned	Tiny	Remote	Wrong
Watchful	Sore	Unsettled	Subdued	Stabbed	Unimportant	Separate	
Worried	Spiteful	Unsure	Tearful	Tortured	Useless	Shunned	
Wrecked	Sullen		Unhappy	Used	Weak	Unwanted	
	Uptight		Weepy	Wounded	Worthless	Withdrawn	

Eventually, she developed the following:

- *I feel **provoked** that you didn't call because I believe you withhold from me on purpose.*
- *I feel **hurt** that you didn't call because it means you don't care about me.*
- *I feel **alarmed** that you didn't call because I don't trust what you're doing.*

Fortified with her new understanding of herself and her feelings, she can now have a conversation with her partner in which she is able to stay focused and on point, addressing each emotion one at a time. I invite clients to choose one statement as a starting point. Sometimes they pick the one they feel the most strongly about, and other times they pick the sentence they predict will be the least controversial, especially as they are learning this communication technique.

"I feel hurt that you didn't call because it means you don't care about me."

STEP TWO. Now it's time for the receiver of the message to enter the process with good active listening skills. It is important for the listener not to judge, criticize, or hijack the conversation. The receiver must be a neutral observer, mirroring back what the sender said. As the receiver, your goal is to *hear* your partner. Ideally, your tone is open, calm, and understanding. You have good eye contact and body language. Having a third party in the room can be helpful at this step because the receiver isn't always aware of the nonverbal messages he is conveying that sabotage the process, and feedback can be very helpful at this point.

Here is a Step Two response that exemplifies two common mistakes listeners make:

"What I heard you say is that you feel upset when I don't call you because I'm not making time for you during the day. Did I hear that correctly?"

STEP THREE. Very often, the spouse will say *"Yes"* at this point, even though he missed the boat on two accounts. He didn't get the feeling word right (she said "hurt" and he fed back "upset"), and he didn't mirror back accurately her reasoning, that he didn't care about her. What he said may seem highly related to that idea (i.e., if I don't care about you then I don't make time for you), but it wasn't *accurate*. Why then, did she indicate he had heard her accurately? It's the ultimate vote-of-no-confidence in couples communication: HE WAS CLOSE ENOUGH. This says to me (and the partner), *"I just don't expect you to do any better than that."* Yuck! How can you aspire for greatness in your relationship if don't expect more than that in a basic communication exercise?

It's up to the sender to demand accuracy. If he doesn't get it right, understand it's because he needs to develop this skill, and he won't do it if you let him off the hook. Don't let him contort your feelings or explanation. Simply assert, "Not quite; what I said was ..." and return to Step One. The message sender is the gate keeper in Step Three. Eventually, he will mirror back accurately, and that's when he gets the green light to move to step four.

STEP FOUR. The burden now falls to the listener to provide a genuinely empathic response. As the listener, your statement of empathy must be genuine, and it's still not about you or whether your perception of events is consistent with your partner's. You need to express your understanding of *how your partner feels.*

Wrong answer: *"I was in meetings all day earning money so you could sit home on your fat ass watching Oprah."* No empathy, defensive, and insulting. The stage is set for a major escalation.

Better (but still wrong) answer: *"I'm sorry I didn't call, but I was in meetings all day."* Though this sounds lovely, it's a communication hijacking. You've taken the focus off her feelings and on to how you spent your day.

Best answer: *"Although I'm not you and I don't know how you feel, I can imagine it feels pretty terrible to think your own husband doesn't care about you."* BINGO! You kept it about her, you expressed empathy for how she feels, and you demonstrated a generosity of spirit that (hopefully) will be returned to you in kind.

Effective communication is a gift partners give to one another. Successfully navigating through this CAFE exercise deserves a moment of pause and celebration. That final statement of empathy is like a pretty bow on a gift-wrapped package. We're not ready for the bow until the exchange has succeeded, and we're not ready for any other ideas or emotions until we've got the current one wrapped.

When couples engage in this exercise together, each taking turns as the sender and the receiver, it can bring to light and possibly smooth over discrepancies in their emotional functioning and expressiveness. Let's say for example, a couple struggles with communication because the woman tends to get emotional while her husband remains logical and fairly unemotional. This dialogue helps her to be more logical about her emotions and helps him to put some empathy into his logical thinking.

Ultimately, this exercise helps you to really understand your feelings before trying to communicate about them with your partner, and likewise, gives your partner this same opportunity for personal clarity and understanding before communicating his (or her) feelings with you. Once you develop your *intrapersonal* understanding of your feelings, then you can engage *interpersonally*, each inviting the other to join in understanding them, too. If you and your partner can do this without getting defensive, there is almost nothing you couldn't talk about. The stage is set for you to know each other **almost as well** as you know your *selves!*

CONCLUSION

In this chapter, we touched on how well others know you compared to how well you know yourself. The main point is this: **You should know yourself better than anyone else knows you**. Get curious about who you are and what makes you tick. Unpack your feelings and motivations first, and then try to help your partner understand them. The burden should not be placed on a loved one to make sense of feelings that you, yourself, don't understand. Your road to whole will be much smoother if you are willing to take ownership of your *self!*

MYTH 10:
WE CAN GO BACK
TO THE WAY WE WERE

There is a very romantic notion that time heals all wounds. But does it? Really, all time can do is give the wound the *opportunity* to heal, and in the case of emotional pain, what the wound does with the time it has can go either way; the wound *might* heal, but it might fester, become gangrenous, and require amputation.

Time alone will not heal a painful betrayal. On the contrary, here's an example:

Sylvia and Roger's Formula for Disaster
Sylvia was a devoted wife to her husband, Roger. She stepped out of her career to care for their two children, and she supported him however she could, entertaining his work colleagues, managing the home, and attending to their children.

"We had a truly perfect marriage," she said, "full of love, magic, and trust. I totally trusted him. We were the couple others looked up to."

Sylvia was devastated when she saw her husband in a passionate embrace with another woman. Later, when she confronted him, Roger admitted to the affair. After a brief and tumultuous period of questioning their future that included a few nights apart, he returned to the home and the two made a commitment to recapture their "perfect" marriage.

They had seen other couples go through similar heartache, some remaining married and some ending in divorce. They were certain they could get past this and back to their own happier times. Time would heal all. They didn't seek professional help. They counted on their commitment to each other and time.

Taking it upon themselves to charter their course through this rough patch, they agreed to certain ground rules. She could articulate whenever she wanted the truth *that he was an ungrateful pig who didn't deserve such a nice and "perfect" wife, and he had to agree with her while feeling and expressing appropriate levels of shame and guilt. They agreed there was no point in exploring their marriage pre-affair, because, "That had all been a lie," she explained. Further, "There's really nothing of interest from back then, anyway. We were perfect and he screwed it up."*

She didn't see the inconsistency in her own argument, that their marriage had been perfect at the same time it had all been a lie. As far as she was concerned, the problem was the affair, and the solution was maintaining a marriage in which she could torture him with the reality of his own (and significant) shortcomings whenever she felt like it.

Part of the condition of their reconciliation was his willingness to be 100% open and honest with her about anything she asked. This made logical sense to her because she didn't want anyone else in the world to know things about her husband that she didn't know, and that included the other woman. So, if the other woman knew something, Sylvia wanted to know it, too. She asked about the details of the affair, the dirty details — where, when, how often, was-it-good-for-you kind of details. As the affair had gone on for several years, and the other woman had been a bit of an exhibitionist, Sylvia could hardly leave her house without traveling into the scene of one of their sexual encounters. It was as if her entire community had gone from bright colors to shades of grey. She didn't feel safe anywhere, and when she didn't feel safe, she was mean to Roger. They tried for two years to allow the healing process to occur naturally, but the situation was getting worse. Sylvia was increasingly suspicious of Roger's every move, she was anxious and paranoid about who in the community might have seen what, who knew what, and who was gossiping about them.

By the time they came in for professional counseling, they had quite a list of issues:

(1) The conditions in the marriage that led to the affair;
(2) The devastating betrayal of the affair;
(3) Sylvia's traumatic response and anxiety;
(4) Two years of pain, chaos, and emotional abuse.

I MARRIED THE PERFECT PERSON REVISITED

Sylvia's need to be the perfect wife in the perfect marriage certainly fits the *"I Married the Perfect Person"* myth from Chapter 8, but she goes farther than either of the women we met in that chapter, in that she works hard to *project* the image of "perfect family" into the community. Sylvia's thinking resembles a concept in developmental psychology used to describe a feature of adolescent egocentrism called the **Imaginary Audience**. Sylvia puts herself at the center of everyone's stage, believing that others are watching and caring about what she is doing. Sylvia is stuck there, and not only does she play to the imaginary crowd, but like putting on a play, what goes on in front of the curtain is more important than what's behind it. In reality, no one but *Sylvia* is in the theater. They've got their own shows to worry about.

Still, Sylvia is stuck in an adolescent mind-set that makes it more important to appear perfect to her imaginary audience than to be genuine in her relationships with neighbors and friends. Now that the jig is up, Sylvia desperately wants to put things back to where they were before, when everything appeared perfect. What does she gain from this image of perfection and where does it come from?

WHAT'S IN IT FOR HER?

When trying to understand motivation, the first thing to explore is the behavior's reinforcement. In strict *psychologese*, anything reinforcing will sustain or increase behavior; reinforcement can involve getting something good or avoiding something bad. We touched on this concept in Chapter 1 and again in Chapter 9. So for Sylvia, we first have to wonder, **is her behavior being reinforced?** If she continues to do it, then we know it is being reinforced somehow, but **how is it being reinforced?** Is she getting something good or avoiding something bad? Her behavior doesn't seem to be getting her the good stuff, affection from her husband or happiness in her marriage, so it hardly seems likely to be the former. What does her behavior help her to avoid? Controlling her environment and everyone in it is her way of creating safety in her world by avoiding her biggest fear, *unpredictable chaos*. Sylvia is not out to get a thrill from controlling others, despite her efforts to appear happy-go-lucky, she is pretty unhappy. Really, she is just trying to feel safe, which is a big red flag for a family of origin with substance abuse, most likely alcohol.

Indeed, Sylvia's mother was an alcoholic, which helps us to understand her desperate need for control and the appearance of perfection. Coming from a terribly chaotic home, Sylvia vowed she would never subject her children to the same unpredictable and scary environment as the one in which she had grown up. She worked tirelessly to provide her children with one "Hallmark" moment after another. Every holiday was a picture post card; every family outing was an event. She saw any personal criticism as a devastating threat to this family image, so Sylvia worked hard to avoid any situation that might garner the most subtle frown or raised eyebrow.[23]

YOU COMPLETE ME REVISITED

We can also explain Roger and Sylvia's case using the *You Complete Me* myth in Chapter 1, because in many ways, Roger's thrill seeking and chaos completed the picture with Sylvia's ultra conservative and controlling ways. Roger grew up in a home with a single mother who was a bit narcissistic and very open sexually. The environment was nontraditional; for example, sometimes dinner consisted of Jiffy Pop and Tab. Mom was a free-thinking hippy, with a degree in theater arts and a love for life that couldn't be confined by convention. The structure and control that Sylvia offered was appealing to Roger. Likewise, Roger's free spirit was a welcome addition to Sylvia's life. So they began their life together, but eventually the *You Complete Me* myth played out. Sylvia sought to control and contain any unconventional impulses Roger had. Roger, in need of a thrill, became the rebellious teenager, who found covert ways to indulge his sexual impulses.

---

[23] If this sounds like you or someone you love, you might want to check out the available literature on "Adult Children of Alcoholics" (ACOA) and the website www.adultchildren.org.

ROMANTIC VERSUS REALISTIC

The desire to go back to "how it used to be" is romantic but very unrealistic. It comes from a genuine longing to feel happy and safe.

- I want to go back to a time before he broke my heart.
- I want to go back to a time when she was sweet and agreeable.
- I want to go back to a time when conversations were easy.
- I want to date again, to have that feeling of excitement and anticipation.
- I want romance.
- I want to know less about who you really are so that I don't have to confront my tendency to be judgmental.
- I want to have the blissful ignorance of a new relationship, full of promise and hope.
- *I want my fantasy unencumbered by reality.*

One problem with rewinding the clock and going back to an earlier and perhaps more simple time in your relationship, is that if nothing changes, you will be on the same path that brought you to your current predicament. Time alone is not enough to change the quality of your love or your relationship. As Roger and Sylvia remind us, time can make matters considerably worse if destructive patterns are not addressed.

WHY DID YOU MARRY YOUR SPOUSE?

I usually pose this very simple question to couples at our first meeting. *"Why did you marry your spouse?"* The answers are not simple.

She was pregnant.
Making a baby together certainly implies a passionate love relationship, but recall from Chapter 7, that's only one-third of the picture. It does not guarantee emotional intimacy or commitment, and often the focus jumps right from the pregnancy to the wedding to the baby, without addressing these other important areas. It could be that years later, after child rearing has eased up because the kids are older

and more self-sufficient, the couple is looking at one another for the first time as people, not just parents. This is an opportunity to get to know each other all over again.

I wanted to get out of my parents' house.

Really? Marriage to solve a housing issue? What prevented you from moving out before marriage? Economic dependency transferred from parents to spouse is not a great start. If you're considering marriage for this reason, find a friend or two and get out of your parents' home first. Be self-sufficient before jumping into another dependent relationship. If this was you twenty years ago, and now you're trying to figure out if you want to stay married, then you need to accept this dependency was a part of your past, but that doesn't mean it needs to be a part of your future. Be in your marriage because you *choose* to be, and find ways to develop your independence while still honoring your marriage and spouse.

We had been together _____ years, and it was time.

Recall Rebecca from Chapter 2, who said, *"We'd invested (so much) time together, it was time to either break up or get married."* The number of people who get married because they hit an arbitrary deadline might surprise you. I have a simple message for couples who are feeling this way and considering marriage:

If you would be okay with your relationship going either way, then break up.

I know it will be hard, and there are reasons to get married, and you love each other. I get that. But, if you head into a marriage believing you could be happy with or without each other, you simply don't have the momentum to carry you through a lifelong commitment.

If the "It Was Time" argument was your rationale for getting married and now you are years into your union, I do not advocate the quick break up. Once you make the commitment to each other you owe it to yourselves and each other to try to make it work. Like Nadine in Chapter 3, Jay in Chapter 7, and Scott in Chapter 9, many are quick to offer their spouse's issues as the cause of marital problems and avoid taking personal responsibility. In short, they have a problem with their "I Sight." Here is what healthy "I Sight" looks like:

> *"**I** need to take responsibility for my happiness."*
> *"**I** must understand what causes my issues."*
> *"**I** have to love myself and my life so that **I** can be ready share it with another."*

Self-imposed time pressure can also keep you stuck asking the wrong question. I will share my own *"Aha!"* moment as an example.

I was attending a Catholic mass one Sunday, and the priest asked a question during the homily. *"If your doorbell rang, and you opened the door and found Jesus on your step, would you be ready to invite him into your house?"* Sometimes the right message is delivered in the right way at the right time and has the right impact. This was one of those moments for me. I was 26 and single, having just broken up with someone I could have easily married. It occurred to me that I had spent my young adulthood feeling pressure to find a person who would make a good spouse, mindful that time was ticking and wondering, *"Is he the right one? Is **he** the right one?"* Almost instantly, as I sat in that church, I realized I had been asking the wrong question, because even if *perfection, Himself* actually landed on my doorstep, it wouldn't matter if I wasn't ready. The question I should have been asking is, *"Am **I** the right one?"* Am *I* ready to receive the gift of great love in my life? Once I figured out the question, my focus finally shifted to me. I addressed my own "I Sight" and prepared myself to be the right person in the right relationship.

Time, in and of itself, is irrelevant. All it can do is create opportunity to develop your best self and decide if your partner is *the one* for you. Marriage is not like musical chairs, *"Quick! Sit down before all the seats are taken!"* No matter how many years you have invested, only get married if you can't imagine your life without this person in it.

These responses — babies, housing, time — reflect external pressures to get married. But the question wasn't, *"Why did you get married?"* The question was:

"Why did you marry your spouse?"

After a moment of blank stares, clients usually come up with one of two answers, one of them being, *"We loved each other."* But as we saw in Chapter 7, there are different kinds of love, not all of which involve commitment, and not all of which will lead to a successful marriage. The other popular answer is:

"We wanted the same things in life."

When I ask clients to clarify what they wanted in life, the typical responses include having children, having a companion in old age, and having some financial security. These are beautiful aspirations, but they just don't narrow the field of potential life partners particularly well.

When it comes to the question of starting a family, most people are true to their biological drive to have children. Recall Garrett and Gina from Chapter 6. Their entire relationship came down to this shared goal. Who knows how it would have turned out had they been able to naturally conceive their own children. As John Lennon wrote, *"Life is what happens to you while you are busy making other plans."*[24] The bottom line is that *wanting children* does not provide a solid enough foundation on which to build an entire marriage.

As far as the aspiration of having a companion with you in old age goes, again, you've not narrowed the field here, either. Who is going to say they want to get old and die alone? No one I know. Let's face it, you're going to get old either way, so why not do so with a companion rather than without? As an aspiration, it's fine; as a selection criteria for a marriage partner, it's not fine.

Finally, you want to have enough money to live comfortably and with the care you need into old age. Again, a fine aspiration, but it's not specific enough. Everyone wants comfort and care as they age. Don't get me wrong; money is an incredibly important component in marriage, and it's routinely identified in the top three causes of marital strife.[25] If money *is* a part of your selection criteria, it's likely to be a big part. It could be that you want to live luxuriously, enjoy the finer things in life, and die sleeping in designer sheets. Or maybe you're like Dale from Chapter 5, and you select a mate based on a shared

---

[24]This is a lyric from the song "Beautiful Boy (Darling Boy)," which he wrote for his son, Sean. It's similar to a quote attributed to Allen Saunders, whose quote "Life is what happens to us while we are making other plans," appeared in Reader's Digest in 1957.
[25]Time and sex are usually listed as the other two items in the top three causes of marriage problems.

commitment to sacrifice today's comforts for tomorrow's security. Simply wanting financial security is a very superficial aspiration. It's important to be very clear about your lifestyle aspirations, and how you expect them to be funded.

THE WEDDING DAY VERSUS THE LIFETIME COMMITMENT

When couples want to go back to an earlier time in their relationship, that desire stems from a longing to feel good again. Their journey has taken unexpected turns, and it's gotten much messier than they ever imagined it would. It could be that they really want to go back to a time when they put each other first. And it may not take years to get to that place. Meet Carly and Drake, a young couple who fell into the wedding trap.

Carly and Drake: Perfect Wedding/Thwarted Marriage
Even though Carly and Drake grew up ten minutes from each other, they didn't meet until they were both away from home and attending the same university. They were well suited for each other, with similar interests and political views, and they both enjoyed intramural sports and board games. Further, they both wanted to move to the west coast after graduation. They fell in love. The summer before their senior year, he proposed, she accepted, and they looked forward to getting married the following July. They returned to school in the fall, excited to celebrate their news with friends. Her mother attended to wedding details at home. She set up several appointments for them over Thanksgiving break. They met with caterers, photographers, bakers, calligraphers, videographers, DJs, and their minister. By the time they were supposed to meet with Randi, the Keepsake Specialist, Drake was D*O*N*E! He had hardly seen his own family or friends all weekend, and he was having a hard time discerning Maize yellow from Sunglow yellow and a worse time understanding why he needed to care.
They got through the holiday and returned to school. They weren't getting along very well, but before long the winter break was upon them, and it was back home for a series of parties and showers to celebrate their pending union. Gifts started to arrive, and the wedding plans continued to take shape.

The rest of their senior year was a blur. They were both busy with schoolwork and social functions. What little time they had together, they spent talking about the wedding. Carly could tell Drake was getting tired of the whole thing, but she dismissed his disinterest as "a guy thing," and continued full-steam-ahead planning the wedding with her mother.

Finally, the wedding day arrived, and all of the planning paid off. Their wedding was perfect, down to every last detail. Their friends and family were there to witness and celebrate the event. As the reception roared on, Carly and Drake said their good-byes, and took off by limousine to catch their flight to Hawaii for their honeymoon. They arrived at the hotel on Maui, checked in, and discovered Carly's parents had surprised them with an upgraded suite with an ocean view. Carly stood on the balcony, soaking it all in. She turned to invite Drake to come and enjoy the view with her, but as she met his eyes, she could see something was wrong. He stood holding his suitcase next to the door. He looked pale and cold.

"What is it?" she asked.

"I can't do this," he replied.

"Can't do what?" she asked, realizing her heart was now pounding in her chest.

"I don't want this. Any of it. We shouldn't have gotten married. I didn't know how to stop it. I'm sorry. I just can't." The heavy door clicked shut behind him. He left the hotel, took a cab back to the airport, and got on the next flight home. The wedding had been perfect, but there wasn't going to be a marriage.

Reality television has given us stark insight about how wedding planning can disastrously impact the start of a marriage. It can be a very trying time for the most stable of families, the most peaceful of brides. Unfortunately, the frenzy of wedding planning makes it easy to disconnect from each other. The case of Carly and Drake is an extreme example, to be sure, but the disconnect is fairly common. You love each other, you decide to spend your lives together, and then the *transition* from boyfriend and girlfriend to husband and wife interferes with the relationship. All Drake wanted was to have the relationship they had before the engagement. But they couldn't go back.

PRIORITIZING THE RELATIONSHIP

I try to help couples see three parts to their relationship — the *me*, the *us*, and the *you*. A large part of this book has addressed the *me*. "What baggage do I bring to this? How is my stuff interfering with our happily ever after?" It also focused on the *you* in your partner, encouraging you to understand your partner's motives and fears. "What has his journey been like?" "How does her perspective lead to her pain?" When you each carry understanding of your *self* and compassion for your *partner*, then you both can care for the *us*, the relationship that you should both cherish. "We Can Go Back to the Way We Were," really identifies a longing for the *us* that used to be, back to a time when we both saw the *us* as a gift that we treasured. If you keep in touch with the *us* along the way, you will never mourn the loss of an earlier time in your relationship; that treasure will still be an active part of your lives. For many couples, the first time they recall losing sight of the *us* was during their wedding planning. So let's be really clear about how to avoid that. First, you have to keep in mind,

The wedding is just one day.

It should be a beautiful day that means the world to both of you. Still, you should never spend more time preparing for the wedding than you spend preparing for the **marriage**. Focus on the shared life you are co-creating, and the color of the napkins will seem much less important.

Second, stay in touch with each other throughout the planning. Tune in to what your fiancé tells you, and try to stay connected to what he or she may be *trying* to tell you that you're not quite hearing. Use communication tools if you need them, and be sure to set aside plenty of time for private conversation.

Finally, remember that this special event has only two guests of honor — you and your fiancé. Parents, grandparents, siblings, and friends are important, and they can certainly weigh in when you ask for their opinions, but do not let them hijack the process of starting your life together. Get help immediately from a qualified therapist who specializes in family relationships to quell any uprisings among loved ones before they get out of hand and cause long-term rifts in relationships.

CONCLUSION

In this chapter, we've explored the sometimes painful truth that no one can go back in time to an earlier point in life or relationship. Though our journey takes us forward, the past can be alluring. We long for a time before our version of reality was thwarted by new truths or painful discoveries. Our travels are full of missteps, and we often wish we could rewind the clock and avoid self destructive mistakes. If you treat your relationship like a precious gift, you will shelter it from harm. You will not let others interfere with it. Before, during, and after the wedding your relationship will be valued and protected. This is the journey you and your partner can take together.

We have addressed ten myths that can interfere with any couple's *happily ever after*. My hope is that this book inspires you to take a closer look at your *self* and understand the role you have in shaping your relationships, for better and for worse. I have no doubt that you are doing a lot of things right. Perhaps you came across an idea that helps you to examine your areas of growth, as well. We are all works in progress, and it is my hope that you have found something in these pages that inspires you to continue your journey of self-discovery.

Index of Key Names and Terms

Academentia 43
ACOA 126
Active listening 119
Adolescent egocentrism 125
Annual summit 59, **60**
Arrogance 36, **49**, 100
Attachment 81
Banished self 10-11
Baum, Brent 98
Bewitched 109
Big four 32
Blind spots .... ii, 4, 5
Boiling frog 51
Breathing, deep 91
Brown, Les 22
CAFE 115, **116**
Choquette, Sonia 40
Codependence 83
Cognitive dissonance 20
Colbert, Stephen 27
Consummate love 84
Commitment 84
Companionate love 84
Defenses 5, **32**, 89, 108
Desperate Housewives 109
Destructive attachment 83
Distraction 91
Ego 34, **38**, 62
Enmeshment 83
Fatuous love 84
Fear 33
Feeling words 118
Fight or flight response 88
Finding a therapist 23
Freud, Sigmund 34
Games people play 96
Gilligan's Island 108
Grounding skills 91
Guilt 37
Holographic Memory Resolution ... 98
Honey-Do P-List .... iv, 31
H.O.T. brain 88
Humility 36
Imaginary audience 125
Inner parts 34

Intake session 24
Intimacy 84
Jerry Maguire 1
Johnny Bravo 18
Kübler-Ross, Elisabeth 46, **76**
Lennon, John 130
Lerner, Harriet 9
Living your spirit 40
Love as attachment 81
Mammalian brain 88
Metacognition 18
Neocortex 88
OCD 20
Operant conditioning 114
Parental attachment 81
Passionate love 84
Perfection 30, **95**
Personality origins 3
Personality states and traits 2, 3
Practice imperfection 102
Projecting/projection ... **18**, 85, 100
Punishment 8
Real versus ideal self 99, **102**
Reinforcement 125
Rogers, Carl 102
Romantic love 84
Rubin, Zick 81
Scripts 16
Self-talk 92
Shame 34
Should -ing/s on **34**, 36, 38, 114
Stages of grief 55, 76
    Acceptance 78
    Anger 77
    Bargaining 77
    Denial 77
    Depression 78
Staying together for the kids 74
Sonny and Cher 75
Sternberg, Robert 84
Therapeutic alliance 24
Transactional analysis 34
Transition twister 76, **79**
Triangular theory of love 84
Truthiness 27

Index of Case Studies

Myth 1: You Complete Me
    Marguerite and Evan: ½ x ½ = ¼ 9

Myth 2: Marriage Will Change Him
    Rebecca and Jesse: The Power of the Script.. 16
    Abby Edits the Script.. 20

Myth 3: If He Would Be Perfect, I Would Be Happy
    Ben, Nadine, and the Honey-Do P-List 31

Myth 4: The Barter Economy Marriage
    Harriet and Edward: A Lopsided Agreement 43

Myth 5: We'll Be Happy When We Get There
    Barry and Tina: An American Dream Goes Bust 54
    Dale and Dora: Scrounging for Security.. 56

Myth 6: Children Will Bring Us Closer Together
    Estelle and Chad: Children Will Keep Him Home 68
    Garrett and Gina's Perfect Plan 71
    Lindsay's Transition Twister.. 76

Myth 7: Love Will Keep Us Together
    Jay and Jessica: Bad Habits in Love... 82
    Connor and Elaine: Understanding Rage... 88

Myth 8: I Married the Perfect Person
    Roy and Mandy: A Game of Blind Man's Bluff 97
    Tammy and Billy: A Game of Liar's Dice 100

Myth 9: He Knows Me Better Than I Know Myself
    Scott's Blame: Better Out than In... 108
    Leticia and Jillian: A Truth Revealed 110
    Jack and Jane: I'll Have What He's Having 112

Myth 10: We Can Get Back To the Way We Were
    Sylvia and Roger's Formula for Disaster 123
    Carly and Drake: Perfect Wedding/Thwarted Marriage 131